Litigating in Federal Court

Litigating in Federal Court:

A Guide to the Rules

Ann E. Woodley

Associate Professor of Law
The University of Akron
School of Law

Carolina Academic Press
Durham, North Carolina

ISBN 0-89089-970-3
LCCN 99-65881

Cover illustration by Ralph Solonitz

Carolina Academic Press
700 Kent Street
Durham, North Carolina 27701
Telephone (919) 489-7486
Fax (919) 493-5668
Email: cap@cap-press.com
www.cap-press.com

Printed in the United States of America

Contents

PART II: Document Drafting Checklists

Preface

After working with the Federal Rules of Civil Procedure for many years — as a federal district court judicial law clerk, a commercial litigator in Washington, D.C., and a law professor — I have developed some expertise in understanding and explaining the interrelationship of the applicable rules for each stage of federal court litigation. The Federal Rules of Civil Procedure (FRCP) are not sufficiently organized or cross-referenced to allow law students or litigators to easily understand the relationships between them or to make sure that all relevant rules have been consulted. Based upon my experience and my "big picture" view of the procedural rules, I have drafted the charts and checklists in this book in an attempt to help remedy this deficiency.

This book is divided into two parts. The first part of the book covers all of the stages of federal court litigation, including a brief explanation of each stage and one or more charts showing the applicable rules and their relationship to each other. (There are a total of 32 charts in this section.) The second part of the book contains 21 checklists for drafting most of the documents used in the pretrial process. These checklists include citations to the basic relevant rules as well. (*Note*, however, that the charts and checklists contained in this book also include some sources other than the FRCP — including federal statutes, common law, and general accepted practice.)

I would like to thank all of my Civil Procedure and Pretrial Advocacy students at The University of Akron School of Law who have motivated me to think about how to explain the relationships between the applicable rules — and particularly those students who have encouraged me to write a book such as this one. I also welcome any feedback on this book so that it can be improved for future editions.

Fall 1999   Ann E. Woodley

About the Author

Ann E. Woodley is an Associate Professor of Law at The University of Akron School of Law, in Akron, Ohio. Professor Woodley has taught Civil Procedure and Pretrial Advocacy at Akron for more than a decade. She also teaches Alternative Dispute Resolution, Mediation Skills, Interviewing and Counseling, and an Employment Discrimination seminar.

Prior to joining the law faculty, Professor Woodley was a commercial and employment litigator at the Washington, D.C. office of Winston & Strawn. Before that she completed a two-year judicial clerkship with the Honorable Carl A. Muecke, (then) Chief Judge of the United States District Court for the District of Arizona, in Phoenix.

Photograph by Joseph Toth, Toth Photo and Video, Stow, Ohio

Litigating in Federal Court

Part I
Litigation Stages

Chapter 1

Overview of Litigation Stages

As stated in the Preface, this book is divided into two parts. The first part of the book covers all of the stages of federal court litigation, including a brief explanation of each stage and one or more charts showing the applicable rules and their relationship to each other. The second part of the book contains checklists for drafting most of the documents used in the pretrial process.

This chapter provides an overview of all of the litigation stages covered in this book. See the chart entitled *Overview of Litigation Stages*, which includes all of the topics — and applicable rules — covered by the succeeding chapters. These topics include: preparation for filing a lawsuit; deciding where the lawsuit should be brought; the determination of applicable law in diversity cases; drafting/serving the Complaint; responding to the Complaint; seeking change of venue; the discovery process; pretrial resolution of cases; dispute resolution alternatives; components of settlements; appealing decisions prior to final judgment; preparing for trial; the basic jury trial stages; post-trial motions; appeals; review by the U.S. Supreme Court; setting aside the judgment; and restraints on subsequent litigation.

(*Note* that in states that pattern their rules of civil procedure after the Federal Rules of Civil Procedure (FRCP), this book can be helpful for state court litigation as well. However, the state versions of the applicable rules should always be checked for minor differences.)

OVERVIEW OF LITIGATION STAGES

Preparation for Filing a Lawsuit
• Client Interview
• Factual Investigation (FRCP 11)
• Legal Research (FRCP 11)
• Developing Theory of Case / Other Strategic Preparation
• Settlement / ADR Options

Deciding Where the Lawsuit Should Be Brought
• Subject Matter Jurisdiction (28 U.S.C. 1331, 1332, 1367, 1441, 1446)
• Personal Jurisdiction
• Venue (28 U.S.C. 1391)
• Other Considerations (e.g. Choice of Law)

The Determination of Applicable Law in Diversity Cases
• Determining Whether Federal or State Law Applies (The Erie Doctrine)
• Determining Which State's Law Applies (Conflict of Laws Principles)

Drafting / Serving the Complaint
(FRCP 4, 8, 9, 10, 11, 12, 18, 20, 23, 38, 65)

Responding to the Complaint
(FRCP 5, 8, 9, 10, 11, 12, 13, 14)
• Pre-Answer Motions or Answer and Claims

Seeking Change of Venue
(FRCP 12(b)(3); 28 U.S.C. 1404, 1406)

The Discovery Process
• Planning Discovery
• Parties' Planning Meeting / Form 35 Report (FRCP 26(f); Form 35)
• Initial Disclosures (FRCP 26(a)(1))
• Initiating Written Discovery Requests (FRCP 33, 34, 36)
• Responding to Written Discovery Requests
• Motions for Physical / Mental Examinations (FRCP 35)
• Taking / Defending / Using Depositions (FRCP 27, 28, 30, 31, 32)
• Seeking Discovery Protection / Sanctions (FRCP 26(c), 26(g), 37)

Pretrial Resolution of Cases
• Default Judgments (FRCP 55)
• Voluntary Dismissal (FRCP 41(a)
• Involuntary Dismissal (FRCP 41(b))
• Summary Judgment (FRCP 56)

OVERVIEW OF LITIGATION STAGES, cont.

Dispute Resolution Alternatives

Components of Settlements

Appealing Decisions Prior to Final Judgment
(FRCP 54(b), 28 U.S.C. 1292(a), 1292(b),
Collateral Order Doctrine, Writ of Mandamus)

Preparing for Trial
- Pretrial Motions (FRCP 21, 42(a), 42(b), 56)
- Pretrial Statements
- Jury Instructions (FRCP 51)
- Final Pretrial Conferences / Pretrial Orders (FRCP 16(d),(e))
- Trial Briefs

Basic Jury Trial Stages
(28 U.S.C. 1861-1871; FRCP 47, 48, 49, 50, 51, 58, 59, 69)

Post-Trial Motions (New Trial Motions / Renewed Motions for Judgment As a Matter of Law)
(FRCP 50, 59, 61)

Appeals
(28 U.S.C. 1291; FRCP 58; F.R. App. P. 4(a); 28 U.S.C. 2111)

Review by the U.S. Supreme Court
(28 U.S.C. 1251, 1253, 1254, 1257)

Setting Aside the Judgment
(FRCP 60(b))

Restraints on Subsequent Litigation
- Claim Preclusion / Issue Preclusion

Chapter 2

Preparation for Filing a Lawsuit

There are five major tasks that must be performed prior to actually filing a lawsuit (assuming a valid cause of action exists). See the chart entitled *Preparation for Filing a Lawsuit*.

The first task, of course, is to interview the client. There are a number of important topics to be discussed at that meeting. The discussion should include the relevant facts; all potential defendants; potential legal theories of recovery (that can be identified at this early stage); potential legal remedies; all possible means of resolving the dispute or solving the problem (including alternative dispute resolution (ADR) methods, such as mediation or arbitration); the nature of the litigation process (to educate your client about its length, cost, risk, public nature, etc.); and, of course, the payment of attorneys' fees and costs.

The second task is to conduct a factual investigation of your client's story. This task continues throughout the pendency of the lawsuit, but sufficient information must be obtained to support your legal theories of the case. And while every competent attorney investigates the facts, this task is also, in effect, required by FRCP 11. Under FRCP 11(b)(3), when you file your Complaint you are certifying to the court that "the allegations and other factual contentions have evidentiary support or, if specifically so identified, are likely to have evidentiary support after a reasonable opportunity for further investigation or discovery." Sanctions can be awarded if this certification is violated. Your factual investigation will include finding out what happened (from sources in addition to your client), who witnessed the events, what relevant documents exist, what physical evidence exists, whether the defendant is solvent, and whether there is insurance coverage. (The insurance information will be provided in the discovery process if it cannot be determined informally.) Of course, after the Complaint has been filed, you will be able to supplement this information through the formal discovery process.

The third task (part of which can be performed simultaneously with the factual investigation) is to perform legal research. This is to determine whether valid legal theories of recovery exist and whether there are legal remedies for your client's claim. Again, all competent attorneys perform this function prior to filing a lawsuit. However, it too is, in effect, required by FRCP 11. Under FRCP 11(b)(2), when you file your Complaint you are certifying to the court that "the claims, defenses, and other legal contentions therein are warranted by existing law or by a nonfrivolous argument for the extension, modification, or reversal of existing law or the establishment of new law." Sanctions can be awarded if this certification is violated as well.

The fourth task is to develop a theory of the case, and to determine where the lawsuit should be brought. It is important to develop a cohesive "story" that will support relief for your client. To determine where the lawsuit should be brought, you must consider the concepts of subject matter jurisdiction, personal jurisdiction, venue, and other considerations. (See Chapter 3.)

Finally, before filing a Complaint, you should explore other possibilities for resolving the dispute. These could include negotiating a settlement, sending a demand letter, or using some alternative dispute resolution (ADR) method. (See Chapter 10, re: dispute resolution alternatives, and Chapter 11, re: components of settlement.)

PREPARATION FOR FILING A LAWSUIT

Client Interview

DISCUSS:

- The Facts?
- Potential D(s)?
- Legal Theory of Recovery?
- Legal Remedy?
- All Possible Means of Resolving Dispute / Solving Problem (including ADR)? Pros / Cons?
- Litigation Process (e.g. risk; length; cost; public nature; stress; etc.)?
- Attorneys' Fees / Costs

Factual Investigation (FRCP 11 (b)(3))

FIND OUT:

- What Happened?
- Witnesses?
- Relevant Documents?
- Physical Evidence?
- Solvent Defendant(s)?
- Insurance?

Legal Research (FRCP 11 (b)(2))

DETERMINE:

- Potential Legal Theory of Recovery?
- Potential Legal Remedy?

Developing Theory of Case / Other Strategic Preparation

DETERMINE:

- Theory of Case / "Story"
- Where Case Can and Should Be Brought (*see chart on deciding where to file suit*)

Settlement / ADR Options

EXPLORE:

- Possible to Settle Now? (*see chart*)
- Try Demand Letter?
- Try ADR Process? (*see chart*)

Chapter 3

Determining Where the Lawsuit Should Be Brought

Determining where the lawsuit should be brought is a critical and complex task. There is one main chart addressing this issue — *Components of the Decision as to Where to File Suit*, as well as two sub-charts — on *Personal Jurisdiction* and *Supplemental Jurisdiction*.

The *Components of the Decision as to Where to File Suit* chart addresses the main considerations involved in deciding whether to file suit in a federal or a state court, as well as determining in which particular court it should be filed. There are three main components of this analysis (which should be analyzed in this order): subject matter jurisdiction, personal jurisdiction, and venue. The first, and most basic, decision to make will be whether to file the lawsuit in state court or federal court. While every state has a court of general jurisdiction, federal courts are of limited jurisdiction. Therefore, it must be determined whether the federal court will have *subject matter jurisdiction* over the dispute. The two main types of federal court subject matter jurisdiction are federal question jurisdiction and diversity jurisdiction. In order to meet federal question jurisdiction (under 28 U.S.C. section 1331), the plaintiff's own cause of action must arise under a federal statute, federal treaty, or provision of the United States Constitution. The basic requirements for diversity jurisdiction are that the parties are of diverse citizenship and that the amount in controversy is more than $75,000. If there are additional claims that do not fall within either of these types of jurisdiction, but are closely related to the claims that do, they may fall within supplemental jurisdiction under 28 U.S.C. section 1367. (See the discussion re: the separate sub-chart on that issue, below.) Keep in mind that even if a case falls within federal subject matter jurisdiction, it may be filed in state court instead (unless it is one of the few types of federal question cases over which federal courts have exclusive jurisdiction, e.g. admiralty, under 28 U.S.C. section 1333, or bankruptcy, under 28 U.S.C. section 1334).

The second consideration in determining where to file suit is whether particular courts will have *personal jurisdiction* over the defendants. In general, the same principles will apply whether the case is filed in federal or state court. (See the discussion of the *Personal Jurisdiction* sub-chart, below.)

The third consideration in choosing a court is where *venue* is proper. This part of the analysis (unlike the first two) will lead plaintiff's counsel to particular county courts (in the state court systems) or to particular district courts (in the federal court system). If the case will be filed in state court, plaintiff's counsel must comply with the specific state venue rules or statutes. If the case will be filed in federal court, there must be compliance with the general federal venue statute (28 U.S.C. section 1391) — or any specific federal venue statute that applies in a particular type of federal question case. Under the general federal venue statute, the requirements vary slightly depending upon within which type of subject matter jurisdiction the case falls. If the case is based solely upon diversity jurisdiction, section *1391(a)* provides that venue is proper *(1)* in a district where any defendant resides (if they all reside in the same state); *(2)* a district in which a substantial part of the events or omissions giving rise to the claim occurred, or a substantial part of property that is the subject of the action is situated; or *(3)* a district in which any defendant is subject to personal jurisdiction at the time the action is commenced, *if* there is no district in which the action may otherwise be brought. Subsection*(3)* is a fall-back provision used only in the event the first two possibilities yield no potential districts where venue is proper. If it is a federal question (or mixed) case, section *1391(b)* sets forth the same requirements except for the last possibility. The third subsection of *1391(b)* states, instead, that venue is proper in a district in which any defendant may be found (again, *if* there is no other district in which the action may otherwise be brought). See, also, subsections (c) (defining a corporate defendant's residence — for the purposes of sections 1391(a)(1) and (b)(1)), and (d) (re: suing alien defendants).

After evaluating subject matter jurisdiction, personal jurisdiction, and venue, plaintiff's counsel will know where the lawsuit *can* be brought. However, as listed on the chart, there are other considerations to be taken into account in order to decide where it *should* be brought. These considerations include: the applicable law (e.g. state substantive law vs. federal procedural law in a federal court diversity case, under *Erie Railroad v. Tompkins*, 304 U.S. 64 (1938) (see Chapter 4); and choice of law principles generally); choice/quality of judges; prior jury verdicts/nature of jury pool; familiarity with rules/local practice; and the location/cost of obtaining evidence and witnesses.

The *Personal Jurisdiction* sub-chart summarizes a very complicated area of the law. Personal jurisdiction is the power of a court to render a valid, binding judgment against a particular defendant. The main issues arise in this area with respect to suits against non-resident defendants. In general, the federal and state courts use the same principles in determining whether personal jurisdiction exists. (The exceptions for federal courts are in federal question cases in which a nationwide service of process statute exists or where FRCP 4(k)(2) applies.) The two basic requirements for personal jurisdiction are *power* and *notice* — and there are *statutory* and *constitutional* aspects of each. With respect to the statutory aspects of the power requirement, a defendant's activities must fall within the provisions of the applicable state long-arm statute. If they do fall within the statute's terms, the constitutional requirements must be met as well. The constitutional requirements are set forth in *International Shoe Co. v. Washington*, 326 U.S. 310 (1945) (and the cases interpreting it). The two components of the *International Shoe* test are *minimum contacts,* and *fair play and substantial justice.* In general, under the minimum contacts portion of the test, it must be determined whether there is specific jurisdiction (where the defendant's contacts with the forum state are only casual or sporadic, but are related to the cause of action) or general jurisdiction (where the defendant's contacts with the forum state are so substantial and continuous that it can be sued for unrelated causes of action). Under the fair play and substantial justice part of the test, the following five factors must be evaluated: (1) the burden on the defendant, (2) the interests of the forum state in adjudicating the dispute, (3) the plaintiff's interest in obtaining convenient and effective relief, (4) the interstate judicial system's interest in obtaining the most efficient resolution of controversies, and (5) the shared interest of the several states in furthering fundamental substantive social policies. See, generally, *Burger King Corp. v. Rudzewicz*, 471 U.S. 462 (1985). (In lieu of meeting the power requirement, the defendant may consent — expressly or impliedly — to the court's exercise of personal jurisdiction over it.)

The statutory part of the notice requirement for personal jurisdiction is met by compliance with the applicable federal service rule (FRCP 4) or the state service rule or statute. Even if that is met, the constitutional standard under *Mullane v. Central Hanover Bank & Trust Co.*, 339 U.S. 306 (1950), must be satisfied as well. Under *Mullane*, the notice must be reasonably calculated, under all the circumstances, to apprise interested parties of the pendency of the action and afford them an opportunity to present their objections.

The *Supplemental Jurisdiction* sub-chart is designed to demonstrate the possible claims that might fall within the federal court's subject matter jurisdiction under 28 U.S.C. section 1367. The general purpose of supplemental jurisdiction is to allow claims that do not fall within the federal court's subject matter jurisdiction to be heard in federal court along with related, jurisdictionally sufficient claims. It is both fair to the litigants and efficient in the use of judicial resources to have the federal court hear the entire case. Prior to the adoption of section 1367 in 1990, these claims fell within two common-law categories formerly called pendent jurisdiction and ancillary jurisdiction. *See*, generally, *Civil Procedure* (2d ed.), by Friedenthal, Kane and Miller (West Publishing Co., 1993), at pp. 63-75. Both concepts involve claims that are closely related to the main, jurisdictionally sufficient claims in a federal court case. But they arise under different circumstances. Traditionally, *pendent jurisdiction* allows a plaintiff who has a substantial federal question claim to join, in the original federal court Complaint, related state law claims against non-diverse defendants. This was later expanded to include (and explicitly allowed under section 1367) pendent *party* jurisdiction — where the related state law claim is brought against a different defendant. (See Roman Numerals I and II of the Supplemental Jurisdiction sub-chart.) *Ancillary jurisdiction* traditionally allowed a defendant (or a party acting defensively) to expand the scope of the initial, jurisdictionally sufficient action (either federal question or diversity) by asserting related, but jurisdictionally insufficient claims against another defendant, the plaintiff, or third parties. The most common uses of ancillary jurisdiction are to provide subject matter jurisdiction for compulsory counterclaims, cross-claims, or third-party claims (and variations thereof). (See the examples under Roman Numeral III of the Supplemental Jurisdiction sub-chart showing such defensive use. *Note*, however, example III(C)(5), where a *plaintiff's* claim against a third-party defendant was held *not* to be a permissible use of ancillary jurisdiction. See *Owen Equipment & Erection Company v. Kroger*, 437 U.S. 365 (1978).) In general, under section 1367, as long as the (otherwise) jurisdictionally insufficient claims fall within the above-mentioned circumstances (either pendent or ancillary jurisdiction), and are sufficiently related to the main claims, supplemental jurisdiction will exist over them. The relatedness test has been expressed as forming "part of the same case or controversy under Article III of the United States Constitution" (section 1367(a)), as deriving from a "common nucleus of operative fact" (*United Mine Workers v. Gibbs*, 383 U.S. 715 (1966)), and as "arising out of the transaction or occurrence that is the subject matter of the opposing party's claim" (see the federal joinder rules). *Id.*

COMPONENTS OF THE DECISION AS TO WHERE TO FILE SUIT

(e.g. federal vs. state court; which federal or state court)

Three Main Components of Analysis (in this order)

1. SUBJECT MATTER JURISDICTION	2. PERSONAL JURISDICTION	3. VENUE
State Court: Every state has a court of general jurisdiction	**State Court:** *(see separate sub-chart)*	**State Court:** *(see applicable state venue rules or statutes)*
OR	**OR**	**OR**
Federal Court: Two main types:	**Federal Court:** (generally the same rules as in state court) *(see separate sub-chart)*	**Federal Court:** 28 U.S.C. 1391*

1. SUBJECT MATTER JURISDICTION

Federal Court:
Two main types:

• **Federal Question** (28 U.S.C. 1331) (actions arising under federal Const., laws or treaties)

OR

• **Diversity** (28 U.S.C. 1332)
- P(s) and D(s) citizens of different states

AND
- amount in controversy more than $75,000.

(if also have related, jurisdictionally insufficient claims, check for *Supplemental Jurisdiction* (28 U.S.C. 1367)

(see separate sub-chart)

(If case meets federal jurisdiction requirements but was filed by plaintiff in state court first, may be able to *remove* it to federal court; see 28 U.S.C. 1441, 1446)

> *(Check to see if federal courts have exclusive jurisdiction, e.g. 28 U.S.C. sections 1333 and 1334)*

3. VENUE

If diversity case *(a), district*

(1) where any D resides (if all Ds in same state)

(2) in which substantial part of events / omissions occurred (or relevant property exists)

(3) where D subject to personal jurisdiction (*if* no other district)

If federal question / mixed case *(b)*, same standards as **(1)** and **(2)** above, but **(3)** is where any D may be *found* (*if* no other district)

(See subsection (c) defining corp. D's residence; and (d) re: suing aliens)

(*Note that if federal question case, check for specific federal venue statute)

COMPONENTS OF THE DECISION AS TO WHERE TO FILE SUIT, cont.

4. OTHER
   CONSIDERATIONS

   - **Applicable Law?**

     - (in diversity case)
       federal procedural law
       vs. state substantive law?
       (The Erie Doctrine) (See charts.)

     - which *state's* substantive law?

   - **Choice / quality of judges**

   - **Prior jury verdicts /
     nature of jury pool**

   - **Familiarity with rules /
     local practice**

   - **Location / cost of obtaining
     evidence, witnesses**

PERSONAL JURISDICTION

POWER
(or Consent)

NOTICE
(and Opportunity
to Be Heard)

Statutory
(state long-arm
statute or rule)

Constitutional
(*International
shoe* and
progeny)

Statutory
(state service
statute or rule,
or FRCP 4)

Constitutional
(*Mullane*)

(or, if fed. Q case in
federal court, possibly
use 5th Amend. and:

• federal nationwide
  service of process
  statute

OR

• FRCP 4(k)(2) alien
  D / fed Q exception)

SUPPLEMENTAL JURISDICTION
(28 U.S.C. 1367)

(where related claims can be heard in federal court even
though there is no independent jurisdictional basis for
them—if they are part of the "same case or controversy")

P
(OH) ——————————→ **D**   (Normal lawsuit)
                    (PA)

I. Pendent (Claim) Jurisdiction (former name)

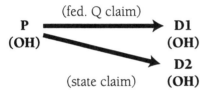

(fed. Q claim)
P ═════════→ **D**
(OH) ═════════→ **(OH)**
(state claim)

II. Pendent (Party) Jurisdiction (former name)

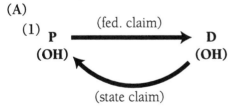

(fed. Q claim)
P ═════════→ **D1**
(OH)   **(OH)**

                D2
(state claim)   **(OH)**

III. Ancillary Jurisdiction (former name)

(A)

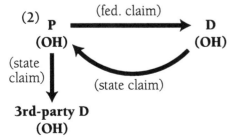

(1)   (fed. claim)
P —————————→ **D**   **Compulsory Counterclaim**
(OH) ⟵——————— **(OH)**   (FRCP 13(a))
      (state claim)   (but need independent
                               basis for jurisdiction if
                               permissive counterclaim)

(2)   (fed. claim)
P —————————→ **D**   **Plaintiff's Third-Party**
(OH) ⟵——————— **(OH)**   **Complaint Arising Out of**
(state   **Compulsory Counterclaim**
claim)   (state claim)   (FRCP 14(a))

3rd-party D
(OH)

SUPPLEMENTAL JURISDICTION, cont.
(28 U.S.C. 1367)

III. Ancillary Jurisdiction (cont.)

(B)

P → D1 & D2   Cross-Claim
(OH)   (PA)   (PA)   (FRCP 13(g))

(C)

(1)

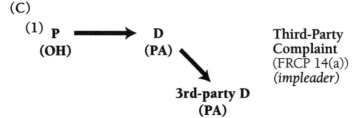

P → D   Third-Party
(OH)   (PA)   Complaint
(FRCP 14(a))
(*impleader*)

3rd-party D
(PA)

(2)

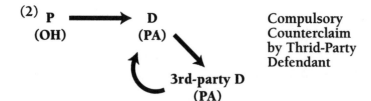

P → D   Compulsory
(OH)   (PA)   Counterclaim
by Thrid-Party
Defendant

3rd-party D
(PA)

(3) (probably)

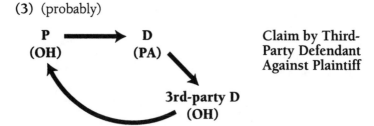

P → D   Claim by Third-
(OH)   (PA)   Party Defendant
Against Plaintiff

3rd-party D
(OH)

SUPPLEMENTAL JURISDICTION, cont.
(28 U.S.C. 1367)

III. Ancillary Jurisdiction (cont.)

(C)

(4) (possibly)

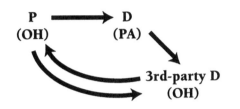

Claim by Third-Party Defendant Against Plaintiff and Plaintiff's Compulsory Counterclaim

(5) ***NOT: (see *Owen Equipment & Erection Co.
v. Kroger*, 437 U.S. 365 (1978))

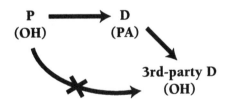

Plaintiff's Claim Against Third-Party Defendant

Chapter 4

The Determination of Applicable Law in Diversity Cases

Before initiating an action in federal court that is based upon diversity jurisdiction (under 28 U.S.C. section 1332), it should be determined what law will apply in the case. (Obviously if the case is filed under federal question jurisdiction, under 28 U.S.C. section 1331, federal law will apply.) See the first chart on determining the applicable law in diversity cases, subtitled *The Basic Components of the Decision (The Erie Doctrine; Choice of Law Principles).*

The first consideration is whether state or federal law will apply. Under the doctrine initially set forth in *Erie Railroad v. Tompkins,* 304 U.S. 64 (1938), in a federal court diversity action state substantive law and federal procedural law will be applied. Unfortunately, it is not always clear whether a particular state law, rule or practice is considered "substantive" or "procedural." If such an issue will be raised, the analysis described below (as illustrated by the second chart in this chapter) must be used.

A second consideration, after determining whether a state law will apply in the case, is *which* state's law? The general rule is that the substantive law of the state where the federal court sits is applied. However, part of that state's law are the conflict of laws principles — which may lead the court to apply the law of another state. (See the chart for examples.)

Third, the *content* of the state law must be determined. A federal court deciding a diversity case is supposed to sit as if it is the highest state court in that state. So if the highest state court has recently spoken on the precise question at issue in a particular setting (or there is

25

an applicable and clear state statute or state constitutional provision), the duty of the federal court to determine and apply state law is easily met. But if this is not true, then the federal court must attempt to predict what the highest state court would decide if the case came before it today. Sometimes federal courts attempt to avoid deciding novel state law issues by using a *certification* procedure, if available, or by *abstaining* from making such decisions, or by *staying* a federal court action while a state court action proceeds. Under a certification procedure, the federal court asks the state supreme court for an answer to a question about state law. Under the doctrine of abstention, if a plaintiff starts a case in federal court with both federal and state claims, the federal court can hold off deciding the federal claims (or abstain), while the plaintiff goes to the state court to get the state claims decided. Finally, where parallel state and federal court actions are proceeding, the federal court could voluntarily stay (temporarily stop) or dismiss the federal court action.

The second chart on this topic illustrates the application of the *Erie* doctrine in depth — after the U.S. Supreme Court's decision in *Hanna v. Plumer*, 380 U.S. 460 (1965) (as explained below). See the chart on determining the applicable law in diversity cases subtitled, *The Erie Problem in Depth (Distinguishing Between Substantive and Procedural Law)*. Remember that the general *Erie* issue is: When must a state law or practice be applied in a diversity action in a federal district court? We know that a federal court deciding a diversity case is supposed to rely upon *state substantive law* and *federal procedural law*, but the terms "substantive" and "procedural" are labels we apply *after* we do the appropriate analysis (in unclear situations).

When competing state and federal laws, rules or practices exist, the test for determining which applies (after *Hanna*) is as follows. If there is an applicable *state* law, rule or practice, you first ask whether there is a similar or competing federal law, rule or practice (or the absence of such a practice in federal courts). If there is, you ask whether an actual Federal Rule of Civil Procedure (or Federal Rule of Appellate Procedure, where applicable) governs the practice under consideration in the particular case. If yes (see the left side of the chart), then ask whether there is a direct conflict between the federal rule and the state law (or rule or practice). If there is a direct conflict, there are two inquiries. The first is whether the federal rule is a valid exercise of power under the Rules Enabling Act. (Under the Rules Enabling Act, 28 U.S.C. section 2072, the U.S. Supreme Court has the power to prescribe, by general rules, the practice and procedure of the federal district courts. The test, under *Sibbach v. Wilson & Co.*, 312 U.S. 1 (1941), is whether the rule really regulates *procedure* — the judicial process for enforcing rights and duties recognized by substantive law and for justly administering remedy and redress for disregard or infraction of them. And the Court in *Hanna* suggests that in virtually all cases an actual Federal Rule of Civil Procedure is presumed to be a valid exercise of the Supreme Court's authority to promulgate procedural rules for the federal courts.) If that test is met, the second question is whether the Rules Enabling Act itself is constitutional (under Article III federal judicial power), which the Supreme Court has, to date, answered in the affirmative. On the other hand, if there is no direct conflict between the Federal Rule of Civil Procedure and the state law (or rule or practice), there are several possibilities. For instance, if the federal rule is discretionary and the state law is mandatory, then you can apply the state law. Or, if the state law has additional requirements that can be followed without doing violence to the federal rule (in other words, superimposing the additional state requirements without interfering with the application of the federal rule), then you can apply both of them in the particular case.

If, however, the federal/state conflict concerns a *federal practice* not mandated by the rule (a pure *Erie* issue) (*or the absence of a practice* in the federal courts when there *is* one in the state courts), then you must use the reformulated outcome-determinative test. (The outcome-determinative test in *Guaranty Trust Co. v. York*, 326 U.S. 99 (1945), was altered by the Court in *Hanna*.) You test the competing state and federal practices against the *twin aims* (or policies) of the *Erie* decision itself:(a) discouragement of forum-shopping, and (b) avoidance of inequitable administration of the laws. With respect to forum-shopping, the question is whether the plaintiff would actually choose the federal court if they thought the federal court would not enforce the state practice in question. With respect to avoidance of inequitable administration of the laws, the question is whether failure to enforce the state practice in federal court would make so important a difference to the character or result of the litigation that it would unfairly discriminate against citizens of the forum state. So, in other words, you ask if a federal court disregards a law of a state that would be applied in a state court action, would that encourage forum-shopping and/or result in the inequitable administration of the laws? And, finally, since the *Hanna* decision did not clearly reject the balancing test from *Byrd v. Blue Ridge Rural Electric Cooperative*, 356 U.S. 525 (1958), it might be appropriate also to consider the significance of the policies behind the competing state and federal practices. The bottom line is that if adhering to the federal practice does *not* encourage forum-shopping, and does *not* result in the inequitable administration of the laws (and the policy behind the state practice is weaker than or equal to the policy behind the federal practice), then the federal law or practice should be applied in the federal court diversity action. If these factors point in conflicting directions, they must be weighed against each other to make a final determination. Note that if the federal law or practice prevails, that means that it is considered "procedural" under the *Erie* doctrine.

Also note that if a federal *statute* is involved (rather than a federal rule, practice, or absence of practice), see *Stewart Organization, Inc. v. Ricoh*, 487 U.S. 22 (1988), where the U.S. Supreme Court held that a federal statute should prevail over a competing state law where the federal statute is broad enough to cover the issue and is a valid exercise of Congress' authority under the U.S. Constitution.

The Determination of Applicable Law in Diversity Cases
THE BASIC COMPONENTS OF THE DECISION (THE ERIE DOCTRINE; CHOICE OF LAW PRINCIPLES)

Federal Subject Matter Jurisdiction

Diversity Cases   Federal Question / Other Cases
                         (apply federal law)

ASK:

1. Does state or federal law apply?

If the state law is deemed to be substantive, it applies.

(You apply state substantive law and federal procedural law.

If there is a question as to whether the law is substantive or procedural, use the outcome-determinative test, as reformulated by *Byrd* and *Hanna*. If a federal rule applies, see *Hanna*; if a federal statute applies, see *Stewart*.) (See separate chart.)

2. If state law applies, which state's law? (And is there a conflict of laws problem?)

Examples:

#1. P   vs.   D   (diversity case filed in Ohio federal court)
   (NY)   (OH)

(case arising out of car accident in Ohio)

Apply the state law of the state in which the federal court sits—here, Ohio state law.

#2. P   vs.   D   (diversity case filed in Ohio federal court)
   (NY)   (OH)

(case arising out of car accident in New York)

Apply the state law of the state in which the federal court sits—here, Ohio state law.

But since events cross state lines, apply Ohio's conflicts of law rules—which may lead to the application of N.Y. tort liability law (place of injury).

The Determination of Applicable Law in Diversity Cases

THE BASIC COMPONENTS OF THE DECISION (THE ERIE DOCTRINE; CHOICE OF LAW PRINCIPLES), cont.

3. If state law applies, what is the content of that law?

(The federal court is sitting as if it is the highest state court in that state.

If there is a recent state Supreme Court opinion (or state statute or state constitutional provision) exactly on point, just apply that law.

Otherwise, the federal court must attempt to predict what that state Supreme Court would decide if this case was before it today.

Federal courts sometimes attempt to avoid deciding novel state law issues by using a *certification* procedure, if it is available, or by *abstaining* from making such decisions, or by *staying* a federal court action while a state court action proceeds.)

The Determination of Applicable Law in Diversity Cases
THE ERIE PROBLEM IN DEPTH (DISTINGUISHING BETWEEN SUBSTANTIVE AND PROCEDURAL LAW)

If Applicable State Law, Rule, or Practice

↓

Similar or Competing Federal Law, Rule or Practice
(or Absence of Such Practice in Federal Courts)?*

Federal Rule

Federal Law or Practice
(or absence of practice)

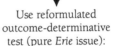

direct conflict with state law?

↓

If yes, ask:

(1) is federal rule a valid exercise of power under the Rules Enabling Act? (i.e., does it concern practice and procedure for federal courts? [*Sibbach*])

AND

(2) is the Rules Enabling Act Constitutional (under Art. III federal judicial power)?

[Validity of federal rules is almost presumed]

If yes, apply federal rule

no direct conflict with state law?

↓

e.g.,

(1) if federal rule is discretionary and state rule is mandatory, **then can apply state law**

OR

(2) if state law has additional requirements that can be followed without doing violence to the federal rule, **then can apply both**

Use reformulated outcome-determinative test (pure *Erie* issue):

(1) Test competing state and federal laws / practices against the twin aims of *Erie*—

   (a) discouragement of forum shopping

   AND

   (b) avoidance of inequitable administration of the laws

[**(2)** and maybe use the *Byrd* balancing test]

(e.g., If adhering to the federal law / practice does not encourage forum shopping and does not result in the inequitable administration of the laws [and the policy behind the state practice is weaker than / equal to the policy behind the federal practice], federal law / practice should prevail. Note: If federal practice prevails, that means it is "procedural.")

(Need to weigh factors)

[*If federal statute, see *Stewart Organization, Inc. v. Ricoh*, 487 U.S. 22 (1988), where the Court held that a federal statute should prevail over a competing state law where the federal statute is broad enough to cover the issue and is a valid exercise of Congress' authority under the U.S. Constitution.]

Chapter 5

Initiating the Lawsuit

The next stage of a federal lawsuit is to actually initiate the action, by drafting, filing, and serving the Complaint.

The first chart, on *Drafting a Complaint*, contains all of the potentially applicable rules (as well as the defendant's potential defenses) that plaintiff's counsel should consider when drafting his or her Complaint. The primary pleading rule applicable to Complaints is FRCP 8(a). Under that rule, there are three basic requirements for a federal court Complaint. The first requirement is that the Complaint include "a short and plain statement of the grounds upon which the court's jurisdiction depends..." This refers to the court's subject matter jurisdiction (generally federal question, under 28 U.S.C. section 1331, or diversity, under 28 U.S.C. section 1332 — and possibly also supplemental jurisdiction, under 28 U.S.C. section 1367). Because federal courts are of limited jurisdiction, it is the plaintiff's burden to demonstrate that the federal court has the power to decide his or her case. The second requirement is that the Complaint contain "a short and plain statement of the claim showing that the pleader is entitled to relief." This is known as "notice pleading" and it differs from the requirements in the state courts that still use the more detailed "code pleading" system. Plaintiffs in federal court simply need to include enough allegations to put the defendant on notice as to the claim for relief they are making. The final requirement is that the Complaint include "a demand for judgment for the relief the pleader seeks." The Complaint need not include a specific dollar amount (except to show, in a diversity case, that the amount in controversy requirement has been met), but it must indicate the type of relief sought (e.g. damages, injunctive relief, etc.). (*Note*, however, that under FRCP 54(c), a plaintiff can recover a final judgment that differs in kind or amount from what was requested in the Complaint — unless the plaintiff has obtained a default judgment.) (See, also, the second page of this chart which refers plaintiffs' counsel to specific additional rules re: pleading special matters (FRCP 9), joining additional claims or parties (FRCP 18, 20), class actions (FRCP 23), demanding a jury trial (FRCP 38), and seeking temporary restraining orders and preliminary injunctions along with the Complaint (FRCP 65).)

This chart also includes mention of other rules that must be complied with in drafting a Complaint in order to avoid sanctions or dismissal. FRCP 11, the sanctions rule, provides that sanctions may be entered against plaintiff and/or his counsel if the Complaint is brought for an improper purpose ((b)(1)), or does not have adequate legal or factual support ((b)(2),(3)). In addition, plaintiff's counsel should consider whether defendant is likely to have valid grounds for making any FCRP 12 Pre-Answer Motions or asserting procedural defenses under FRCP 12(b) or 8(c). If plaintiff's counsel has considered these possibilities ahead of time he or she may be able to make changes to avoid such attacks. Finally, of course, Complaints must comply with the applicable rules of form (FRCP 10).

After the Complaint has been drafted, it must be filed with the court and a copy of it and the Summons must be served upon the defendant. See the description below of the various service methods under FRCP 4, and the accompanying chart.

The second chart, on *Service of the Complaint*, contains all of the methods of service available under FRCP 4. Each method except service by mail involves the service of both the Complaint and the Summons. The first method of service listed is personal service (under FRCP 4(e)(2)), which means physically handing a copy of the Complaint and Summons to the defendant. Any person who is over the age of 18 may perform this task, with the exception of an actual party to the lawsuit (FRCP 4(c)(2)).

A second method of service is to leave a copy of the Complaint and Summons at the defendant's residence, with someone "of suitable age and discretion" who also lives there. Service to a defendant's 16-year-old daughter has been upheld. See *DeGeorge v. Mandata Poultry Co.*, 196 F.Supp. 192 (E.D. Pa. 1961).

A third method of service is by mail, by which plaintiff's counsel is asking the defendant to waive formal service of the Summons. The plaintiff's counsel mails to the defendant a copy of the Complaint, a completed copy of FRCP Form 1-A (Notice of Lawsuit and

Request for Waiver of Service of Summons) and FRCP Form 1-B (Waiver of Service of Summons). If the defendant signs and returns the waiver form (FRCP Form 1-B) within thirty days of the date the request was sent, service has been effected. (The defendant must also file a copy of the response with the court.) Return of the signed waiver form also allows the defendant to respond to the Complaint within sixty days from the waiver request date (rather than the twenty-day time period under FRCP 12). (Note that these time periods are enlarged for defendants served by mail outside any judicial district of the United States.) If the defendant does not return the signed waiver within the thirty-day time period, the plaintiff's counsel must use another method to serve the defendant. The rule allows the court to order the defendant to pay the costs of the second form of service unless "good cause" can be shown for his failure to sign and return the waiver. (Note that the waiver form itself states that it is *not* good cause for a failure to waive service that a party believes that the complaint is unfounded, or that the action has been brought in an improper place or in a court that lacks jurisdiction over the subject matter of the action or over its person or property. The form also states that a party who waives service of the summons retains all defenses and objections — except any relating to the summons or to the service of the summons — and may later object to the jurisdiction of the court or to the place where the action has been brought.)

Other methods of service include using the applicable state service statute or rule in either the state where the suit is brought or the state in which the service will be made (FRCP 4(e)(1)). In addition, there are specific service rules that apply to defendants who have appointed an agent for service of process (FRCP 4(e)(2)), defendants who are in a foreign county (FRCP 4(f)), defendants who are infants (under the age of 18) or incompetents (FRCP 4(g)), defendant corporations or associations (FRCP 4(h)), defendants who are federal agencies, corporations or officers (or the United States itself) (FRCP 4(i)), and defendants who are foreign, state or local governments (FRCP 4(j)).

Note, also, that if service is not made within 120 days after the Complaint is filed, the suit can be dismissed (without prejudice) (FRCP 4(m)).

See, also, checklist #1, entitled *Complaint Checklist*.

DRAFTING THE COMPLAINT

Comply With Pleading Rules (FRCP 8(a))	Comply With Sanction Rules (FRCP 11)	Be Able to Withstand Motions / Defenses	Comply With "Form" Rules (FRCP 10)
Must include: (1) statement of basis for court's jurisdiction (federal SMJ, e.g. Diversity, Federal Question, Supplemental) **AND** (2) short and plain statement of the claim ("notice" pleading) **AND** (3) demand for judgment (remedy sought) *(but see also FRCP 54(c)— under which the final judgment may differ from the demand)*	• no improper purpose, (b)(1) • legal claims warranted by existing law / nonfrivolous argument for change, (b)(2) • factual allegations have evidentiary support (or will have), (b)(3) • (complaint is signed, (a))	• SMJ exists, 12(b)(1) • PJ exists, 12(b)(2) • Venue is proper, 12(b)(3) • Process (summons) is sufficient, 12(b)(4) • Service of process is sufficient, 12(b)(5) • Complaint states a claim, 12(b)(6) • Complaint is suff. specific, definite, 12(e) • No redundant, immaterial, impertinent or scandalous matter, 12(f) • 8(c) Defenses not valid	

See, also:
- FRCP 9—pleading special matters, such as fraud and mistake
- FRCP 18 and 20 re: joining claims / parties
- FRCP 23 re: class actions
- FRCP 38 re: demand for jury trial
- FRCP 65 re: seeking TROs and preliminary injunctions

Note:

- *The Complaint will then be filed / filing fee paid / judge selected by the clerk*

- *A copy of the Complaint and the Summons must be served upon the defendant (see FRCP 4 and separate sub-chart)*

SERVICE OF THE COMPLAINT
(and Summons) (FRCP 4)

PERSONAL FRCP 4(e)(2)	RESIDENCE FRCP 4(e)(2)	MAIL FRCP 4(d)	OTHER METHODS
(hand it to D) (by anyone age 18 or over, except a party —4(c)(2))	(leave it at D's home with someone of suitable age and discretion who is residing there)	(requesting waiver of service of summons) (Send Complaint, Form 1-A, and Form 1-B (*Note:* this alters the D's response time from 20 days to 60 days)	• By any means done in local state courts in same area where case *filed* or where *service is made* (4(e)(1)) • Upon an agent authorized to receive service (4(e)(2)) *See, also:* • 4(f)—persons in foreign country • 4(g)—infants / incompetant persons • 4(h)—corps. / associations • 4(i)—U.S. or its agencies, corps., officers • 4(j)—foreign, state, or local governments

Note 120-day service limitation, FRCP 4(m))

Chapter 6

Responding to the Complaint

There are two basic procedural ways that a defendant can respond initially to a Complaint: (1) file Pre-Answer Motions, or (2) file an Answer (with or without claims). See the chart entitled *Responding to the Complaint*. If the defendant chooses to file Pre-Answer Motions first, it must do so prior to the expiration of the time for filing an Answer (generally within 20 or 60 days of the service of the Complaint). If the Pre-Answer Motions are denied, the defendant must then file an Answer. An additional type of motion that could be filed at this time, where appropriate, is a Motion for Sanctions under FRCP 11.

If the defendant files Pre-Answer Motions under FRCP 12, in general they must include all possible defenses under that rule (see FRCP 12(g)) or they will be waived (see FRCP 12(h)). The possible defenses that may be raised by a Pre-Answer motion are lack of subject matter jurisdiction (FRCP 12(b)(1)), lack of personal jurisdiction (FRCP 12(b)(2)), improper venue (FRCP 12(b)(3)), insufficiency of process (FRCP 12(b)(4)), insufficiency of service of process (FRCP 12(b)(5)), failure to state a claim upon which relief can be granted (FRCP 12(b)(6)), and failure to join a necessary or indispensable party under FRCP 19 (FRCP 12(b)(7)). A motion for more definite statement (under FRCP 12(e)) and a motion to strike (under FRCP 12(f)) are additional possibilities. (If the motions are denied, the defendant must then file an Answer.)

If the defendant, instead, chooses to Answer the Complaint (or must do so later), there are three potential components of the Answer. First, it must contain responses to all of the allegations in the plaintiff's complaint. Under FRCP 8(b), the possible types of responses include admissions, denials, partial admissions or denials, and lack of sufficient knowledge or information sufficient to form a belief as to the truth of the allegation. After the responses have been made, the defendant must also include in the Answer all of its affirmative defenses — or they will be waived. Sources of ideas for affirmative defenses include FRCP 8(c) (a non-exclusive list), FRCP 12(b) (if such defenses have not already been determined by Pre-Answer Motion), and common law. Finally, if appropriate, the Answer should also include any valid claims for relief the defendant may wish to bring. These include counterclaims (claims against the plaintiff, under FRCP 13(a) or (b)), cross-claims (claims against co-defendants, under FRCP 13(g)), or third-party claims (claims against a person the defendant brings into the suit, under FRCP 14). (To make sure that the Answer is timely filed — thus preventing the entry of a default judgment — the defendant should consult FRCP 12(a) and 6.)

Finally, in addition to the Pre-Answer Motions or the Answer, the defendant might choose to file a Motion for Sanctions under FRCP 11. Under FRCP 11, the Complaint can be stricken if it is not signed (FRCP 11(a)), and sanctions can be awarded if any of the FRCP 11(b) certifications have been violated by the plaintiff. These certifications include that the Complaint was not filed for an improper purpose (FRCP 11(b)(1)), that it is warranted by existing law or by a nonfrivolous argument for the extension, modification, or reversal of existing law or the establishment of new law (FRCP 11(b)(2)), and that the factual allegations have evidentiary support or, if specifically so identified, are likely to have evidentiary support after a reasonable opportunity for further investigation or discovery (FRCP 11(b)(3)). (But see the "safe harbor" rule, FRCP 11(c)(1)(A), requiring 21 days' notice to the other side prior to the actual filing of the motion.)

(*Note*: Other rules to consult in this context include FRCP 5 (re: service of all documents after the Complaint); FRCP 7(b) (re: form of motions); FRCP 9 (re: pleading special matters); FRCP 10 (re: form of pleadings); FRCP 11(b)(4) (re: denials in the Answer being warranted on the evidence); and FRCP 12(g) and (h) (re: the consolidation of defenses in the Pre-Answer Motions and the waiver or preservation of certain defenses).)

See, also, checklists #2-4 entitled *Pre-Answer Motions Checklist*, *Responses to Motions Checklist*, and *Answer and Defendants' Claims Checklist*.

RESPONDING TO THE COMPLAINT

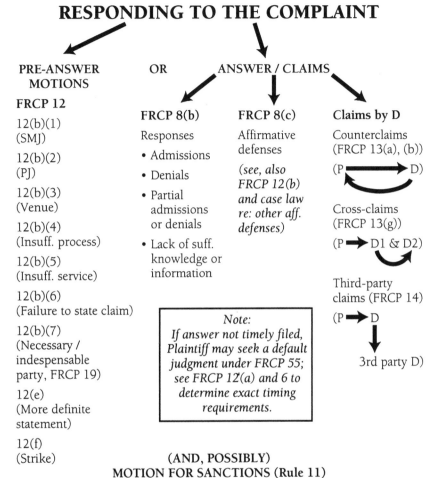

PRE-ANSWER MOTIONS

FRCP 12

12(b)(1)
(SMJ)

12(b)(2)
(PJ)

12(b)(3)
(Venue)

12(b)(4)
(Insuff. process)

12(b)(5)
(Insuff. service)

12(b)(6)
(Failure to state claim)

12(b)(7)
(Necessary / indespensable party, FRCP 19)

12(e)
(More definite statement)

12(f)
(Strike)

OR

ANSWER / CLAIMS

FRCP 8(b)

Responses
• Admissions
• Denials
• Partial admissions or denials
• Lack of suff. knowledge or information

FRCP 8(c)

Affirmative defenses

(see, also FRCP 12(b) and case law re: other aff. defenses)

Claims by D

Counterclaims
(FRCP 13(a), (b))

(P ⟷ D)

Cross-claims
(FRCP 13(g))

(P → D1 & D2)

Third-party claims (FRCP 14)

(P → D)
↓
3rd party D)

> **Note:**
> If answer not timely filed, Plaintiff may seek a default judgment under FRCP 55; see FRCP 12(a) and 6 to determine exact timing requirements.

(AND, POSSIBLY)
MOTION FOR SANCTIONS (Rule 11)

• Not signed (11(a))
• Improper purpose (11(b)(1))
• Not warranted by law (and no basis for change in law) (11(b)(2))
• No evidentiary support (or likely such support) for facts (11(b)(3))

(But see "safe harbor" rule, FRCP 11(c)(1)(A))

(See, also, FRCP 5 (re: service of all documents after the Complaint); FRCP 7(b) (re: form of motions); FRCP 9 (re: pleading special matters); FRCP 10 (re: form of pleadings); FRCP 11(b)(4) (re: denials in Answer being warranted on the evidence); and FRCP 12(g) and (h) (re: the consolidation of defenses in the Pre-Answer motions and the waiver or preservation of certain defenses).

Chapter 7

Seeking Change of Venue

The venue scheme applicable to a particular judicial system normally is adequate to insure that actions are litigated in convenient and sensible places. But a well-functioning venue system also must make provision for *changes* of venue when actions are brought in places that, for one reason or another, are *inappropriate*. See the chart entitled *Seeking Change of Venue*.

Improper Venue

The most obvious situation calling for a change in venue is when the plaintiff brings her federal court suit in a district where venue is *improper*, and the defendant makes a timely objection (e.g. a *12(b)(3)* motion to dismiss). To dismiss the action in every case of this type often might work an injustice (e.g. when the statute of limitations has run).

Federal Court:

In addition to dismissal under FRCP 12(b)(3), a federal court has the power, in the interest of justice, to *transfer* the case to another federal court where venue is proper under 28 U.S.C. section 1406(a). (Dismissal under this statute is also a possibility.)

State Court:

If the case is in state court and venue is improper but would be proper somewhere else in the same state, the state court can *transfer* it to the appropriate county court within the state (since it is a statewide system and it has the power to do so), or it can dismiss the case. If the proper venue is in another state altogether, the court would have to dismiss since it would have no power to transfer the case to another state's court.

Proper, but Inconvenient Venue

But even if the plaintiff's forum choice is *proper* in the sense of meeting the venue requirements, that does not mean that the court chosen is the most appropriate, or even desirable, forum from the standpoint of convenience and efficiency. (Remember that often there are several courts in which venue would be proper.)

Federal Court:

In such a situation, a federal court can either *transfer* the case to another federal court under 28 U.S.C. section 1404(a) (the most usual circumstance), or it can *dismiss* it under the common law doctrine of *forum non conveniens* (upon the condition that it be refiled in the more convenient forum). The latter doctrine applies *if* that other (more convenient) forum is a state court or a foreign court (since the federal court has no power to transfer a case to either of these types of courts).

State Court:

In such a situation, a state court can either *transfer* the case to another court within the same state, or it can *dismiss* it under the common law doctrine of *forum non conveniens* (upon the condition that it be refiled in the more convenient forum). The latter doctrine applies *if* the more convenient forum is in another state or it is a federal court or a foreign court (since the state court has no power to transfer the case under these circumstances).

SEEKING CHANGE OF VENUE

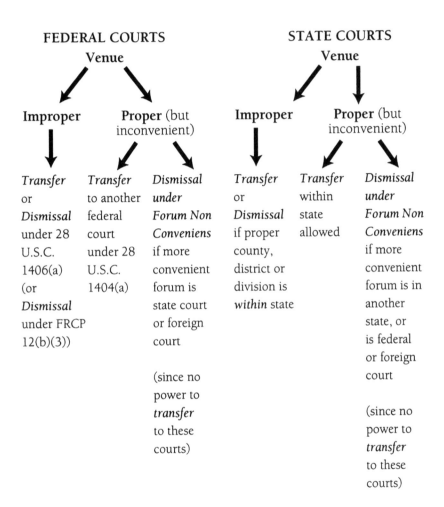

FEDERAL COURTS

Venue

Improper

Transfer or Dismissal under 28 U.S.C. 1406(a) (or Dismissal under FRCP 12(b)(3))

Proper (but inconvenient)

Transfer to another federal court under 28 U.S.C. 1404(a)

Dismissal under Forum Non Conveniens if more convenient forum is state court or foreign court

(since no power to transfer to these courts)

STATE COURTS

Venue

Improper

Transfer or Dismissal if proper county, district or division is within state

Proper (but inconvenient)

Transfer within state allowed

Dismissal under Forum Non Conveniens if more convenient forum is in another state, or is federal or foreign court

(since no power to transfer to these courts)

Chapter 8

The Discovery Process

The discovery process is the formal, fact-gathering method in lit-igation. There are eight charts in this chapter that illustrate the var-ious aspects of the process in the federal courts.

The first task to undertake in this area is to *plan* the discovery that will be taken in the case. See the chart entitled *Planning Dis-covery*. There are two different types of discovery planning — cre-ating an internal discovery plan for your own client, and preparing for the adoption of a joint or court-ordered discovery plan. The first task is necessary so that you can make sure that you obtain all of the relevant information necessary to support your claims and de-fenses — and in the most efficient way possible. The second task is necessary because in the courts that follow FRCP 26(f) (Meeting of Parties; Planning for Discovery), you will have to meet with oppos-ing counsel and agree on all of the elements listed in Form 35 (Re-port of Parties' Planning Meeting). Since it is likely that the court will incorporate your agreed-upon limitations into a court order, it is important that you have prepared in advance for this meeting. Even in courts that do not (as yet) follow FRCP 26(f), many judges hold scheduling or discovery conferences and expect attorneys to agree upon limitations in this area.

The next task in the discovery process is to attend the Parties' Planning Meeting (under FRCP 26(f)) (assuming that the court your case is in follows this rule), and to make the subsequent Form 35 re-port. See the elements of these tasks listed in the chart entitled *Par-ties' Planning Meeting/Form 35 Report*.

The third discovery task is to serve initial disclosures upon op-posing counsel (assuming that the court has not opted out of FRCP 26(a)(1)). This procedure, and the subjects of disclosure, for this controversial, automatic discovery device are set forth in the chart entitled *Initial Disclosures*.

In general, the next phase of discovery is to initiate written discovery requests. These requests include interrogatories (under FRCP 33), requests for production of documents (under FRCP 34), and requests for admissions (under FRCP 36). (It is common to serve requests for admissions at a later point in the case, however, after other discovery has been completed.) Information concerning these requests, and the responses thereto, is contained in the charts entitled *Initiating Written Discovery Requests*, and *Responding to Written Discovery Requests*.

Two other discovery methods are FRCP 35 motions for physical or mental examinations (most commonly used in personal injury actions), and FRCP 30 depositions. The requirements for these methods are detailed in the charts entitled *Motions for Physical/Mental Examinations*, and *Taking/Defending/Using Depositions*.

Finally, in the discovery context, a party may need the assistance of the court for three purposes: (1) seeking protection from discovery, (2) compelling discovery, and (3) seeking discovery sanctions. This more complicated area is addressed in the chart entitled *Seeking Court Assistance in the Discovery Process* and is explained below. The basic method for seeking protection from discovery is to file a *FRCP 26(c)* motion for protective order. Rule 26(c) itself states that such a court order may be entered where good cause is shown and which justice requires to protect a party or person from annoyance, embarrassment, oppression, or undue burden or expense. A non-exclusive list of eight types of protective orders includes orders that the discovery not be had, or that it take place under certain terms and conditions, or that the information revealed be kept confidential. (Note that before such a motion may be filed the movant must, in good faith, confer or attempt to confer with the other affected parties in an effort to resolve the dispute without court action.) A party can also make a Rule 26(c) motion for protective order to limit the frequency or extent of use of the discovery methods under FRCP 26(b)(2) (if one of the three enumerated grounds for such a limitation is present). These latter types of orders also can be entered on the court's own motion after reasonable notice to the parties. Finally, FRCP 30(d)(2) and (3) provide for some court protection in the deposition context. Under FRCP 30(d)(2), a court may, by order or local rule, protect a party by limiting the time permitted for the conduct of a deposition. Under FRCP 30(d)(3), if a deposition is being conducted in bad faith or in such manner as unreasonably to annoy, embarrass, or oppress the deponent or party, the court may order the officer to cease forthwith from the taking of the deposition, or may limit the scope and manner of the taking of the deposition as provided in FRCP 26(c) (the protective order rule).

The second type of assistance a party might seek from the court is an order compelling specific discovery from the other side (if the discovery requests or questions have not yielded all of the appropriate information). The basic method for obtaining such an order is to file a motion to compel under FRCP 37(a). The only allowable sanctions in this context are the expenses of the motion (under FRCP 37(a)(4)). An additional type of motion to compel discovery that applies in the deposition context is a motion for additional time (if needed for a fair examination of the deponent or if the deponent or another party impedes or delays the examination) under FRCP 30(d)(2).

The third type of assistance a party might seek from the court in the discovery context is an award of sanctions. There are a number of possible sanction rules that apply in particular circumstances. Sanctions can be awarded under FRCP 37(b) if the court has issued an order compelling the discovery (e.g. pursuant to a FRCP 37(a) motion) and the party has failed to comply with that order. There are a variety of possible sanctions, including contempt (the only sanction available against a non-party deponent), an order considering certain facts to be established, an order disallowing the introduction of certain evidence at trial, an order striking pleadings or rendering default judgments, and an order requiring the attorney or party or both to pay the reasonable expenses (including attorneys' fees) caused by the failure. Sanctions also may be awarded under FRCP 37(c) for the failure to make complete and accurate initial disclosures. Also included in FRCP 37(c) are sanctions for failing to admit the genuineness of any document or the truth of any matter as requested under FRCP 36 (requests for admissions) when at trial such document is proven to be genuine or such matter is proven to be true. FRCP 37(d) addresses available sanctions when a *party completely fails* to respond to discovery (e.g. by failing to appear for a deposition, or failing to respond at all to interrogatories or document requests.) This rule is rather powerful since it allows the court to award all possible sanctions under FRCP 37(b)(2)(A),(B), and (C) — without the prerequisite of a violation of a court order. FRCP 37(g) allows sanctions to be awarded when a party or a party's attorney has failed to participate in good faith in the development and submission of a proposed discovery plan as required by FRCP 26(f) (re: the parties' planning meeting). In the context of depositions, FRCP 30(d)(2) and (3) allow for the imposition of sanctions — in addition to the types of orders mentioned above (to allow additional time or to stop the deposition, or limit its scope and manner). FRCP 30(g) allows for an award of sanctions where the party giving the notice of deposition fails to attend, or where a non-party deponent fails to appear because he or she was not subpoenaed. Finally, FRCP 26(g) (the FRCP 11-equivalent for discovery), allows for the imposition of sanctions where the initial disclosures are incorrect or incomplete, or where the discovery requests, responses, or objections violate the certifications listed in FRCP 26(g)(2) (e.g. proper under the law/rules, not for an improper purpose, and not unreasonable or unduly burdensome or expensive).

See, also, checklists #5-17, entitled *Report of Parties' Planning Meeting (Form 35) Checklist, Initial Disclosures Checklist, Interrogatories Checklist, Answers to Interrogatories Checklist, Requests for Production Checklist, Responses to Requests for Production Checklist, Requests for Admissions Checklist, Responses to Requests for Admissions Checklist, Motion for Physical/Mental Examination Checklist, Notice of Deposition Checklist, Joint Deposition Notice/Subpoena Checklist, Preparing a Deposition Outline Checklist,* and *Outline for Preparing a Deponent Checklist.*

PLANNING DISCOVERY

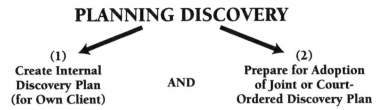

(1)		(2)
Create Internal Discovery Plan (for Own Client)	**AND**	**Prepare for Adoption of Joint or Court-Ordered Discovery Plan**

Explanation:

(1) **Create Internal Discovery Plan (for Own Client):***

- Identify causes of action / defenses of both sides
- Identify all elements of above
- List all factual information necessary to prove claims / defenses
- Decide which discovery devices would better yield such information (taking cost / time into account):
  - Initial Disclosures (from other side) (FRCP 26(a)(1))?
  - Interrogatories (FRCP 33)?
  - Requests for Production (Documents / Tangible Things / Entry Upon Land) (FRCP 34)?
  - Requests for Admissions (FRCP 36)?
  - Motions for Physical / Mental Examination (FRCP 35)?
  - Depositions (FRCP 30)?
- Plan a logical sequence for the use of such devices (e.g. obtain relevant documents prior to deposition so witness can be asked about them there) (also allow for sufficient time to pass between such use in order to accommodate rule restrictions)

(2) **Prepare for Adoption of Joint or Court-Ordered Discovery Plan:**

- In anticipation of Parties' Planning Meeting (FRCP 26(f); Form 35) or other court-ordered discovery conference or order, determine:

  (a) **Reasonable / Beneficial Dates or Time Periods for:**
  - Exchanging Initial Disclosures (FRCP 26(a)(1))
  - Amending pleadings/joining additional parties (FRCP 15; FRCP 20)
  - Response times for Interrogatories (FRCP 33) / Requests for Production (FRCP 34) / Requests for Admission (FRCP 36)
  - Times or intervals for supplementing discovery (see FRCP 26(e))
  - Cut-off of discovery
  - Filing of dispositive motions
  - Service of expert reports (see FRCP 26(a)(2)(B))
  - Filing of final witness and exhibit lists (and objections thereto) (see FRCP 26(a)(3))
  - Final Pretrial Conference (see FRCP 16)
  - Trial (and projected length)

PLANNING DISCOVERY, cont.

(b) Other Limitations, e.g.:
- Subjects of discovery
- Maximum number of Interrogatories (see FRCP 33(a)) / Requests for Production (FRCP 34) / Requests for Admission (FRCP 36)/Depositions (FRCP 30)
- Maximum length of depositions

(c) Whether and When Settlement Attempts Can Be Made / What ADR Procedure(s) to Suggest

(It should also be determined whether to request a court conference prior to the court's entry of a scheduling order.)

** For a more detailed explanation of this process,
see "Strategic Planning in Discovery,"
by Imwinkelried & Blumoff, Trial, August 1987.*

PARTIES' PLANNING MEETING / FORM 35 REPORT

Parties' Planning Meeting ➡️ Report to Court
(FRCP 26(f))   (Form 35)

- Must meet in person
- Must meet as soon as practicable after pleadings filed and, in any event, at least *14 days* before scheduling conference is held or scheduling order due under FRCP 16(b)
- Must attempt to agree on proposed discovery plan in *good faith*
- Must discuss all items to be included in *Form 35 Report* (*see column on right*)

Must include:

- Date, place of FRCP 26(f) meeting / persons attending
- Date of disclosures under FRCP 26(a)(1)
- *Proposed Joint Discovery Plan* (including subjects of discovery; discovery cut-off date(s); maximum number of interrogatories and requests for admission, and response times; maximum number of depositions / length limits; dates expert reports due; times or intervals for supplementing discovery)
- *Other Items* (including whether requesting court conference before scheduling order; month / year pretrial conference requested; cut-off dates for parties to amend pleadings / join parties; cut-off date for filing depositive motions; likelihood of settlement / suggestion of ADR procedures; due dates for filing final witness and exhibit lists, and for objecting to items on such lists; date by which case will be ready for trial; projected length of trial)

INITIAL DISCLOSURES
(FRCP 26(a)(1))

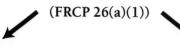

PROCEDURE

- Disclosures are automatic (no request required)
- Must be made within 10 days after Parties' Planning Meeting (FRCP 26(f)) (unless otherwise agreed or ordered by court)
- Must be based on information then reasonably available to party
- Not excused from making disclosures because—
  - investigation of case not fully completed
  - challenging sufficiency of another party's disclosures

  OR

  - another party has not made its disclosures
- Note continuing duty to supplement, under FRCP 26(e)(1)

SUBJECTS OF DISCLOSURE

- **FRCP 26(a)(1)(A)— Witnesses** (persons with discoverable information) (provide name / address / phone no. / subject of information)

  (Note limitation: applies to individuals likely to have discoverable information relevant to disputed facts alleged with particularity in the pleadings)
- **FRCP 26(a)(1)(B)— Documents / Things** (description or copies)

  (Note same limitation as above)
- **FRCP 26(a)(1)(C)— Damage Computation** (and underlying documents)
- **FRCP 26(a)(1)(D)— Insurance Agreements**

INITIATING WRITTEN DISCOVERY REQUESTS*
(Interrogatories; Requests for Production; Requests for Admission)

	Interrogatories (FRCP 33)	Requests for Production (FRCP 34)	Requests for Admission (FRCP 36)
Used for:	• finite types of info (e.g. i.d. of parties, witnesses persons with knowledge; financial info; identification of documents)	• inspection of documents or tangible things, or entry upon land	• obtaining admissions of truth of relevant info (so don't have to prove at trial / to narrow issues) or of genuineness of documents (to be used at trial)
Specific Requirements:	• serve on parties only	• parties or others (if use Rule 45 subpoena for latter)	• serve on parties only
	• must allow 30 days to respond (*but see FRCP 29 re: stipulating changes*)	• must allow 30 days to respond (*but see FRCP 29 re: stipulating changes*)	• must allow 30 days to respond (*but see FRCP 29 re: stipulating changes*)
	• limited to 25 (including all discrete subparts) (without leave of court or stipulation)	• must specify reasonable time, place, manner for production	

INITIATING WRITTEN DISCOVERY REQUESTS, cont.

(Interrogatories; Requests for Production; Requests for Admission)

Interrogatories (FRCP 33) (cont.)

Requests for Production (FRCP 34) (cont.)

Requests for Admission (FRCP 36) (cont.)

Specific Requirements:

- requests must fall within the scope of discovery (*see FRCP 26(b)(1)*—anything not privileged, and relevant to the subject matter of the case—including anything reasonably calculated to lead to the discovery of admissible evidence)

- must be set forth by individual item or category—and described with reasonable particularity

- requests must fall within the scope of discovery (*see FRCP 26(b)(1)*—anything not privileged, and relevant to the subject matter of the case—including anything reasonably calculated to lead to the discovery of admissible evidence)

- requests must fall within the scope of discovery (*see FRCP 26(b)(1)*—anything not privileged, and relevant to the subject matter of the case—including anything reasonably calculated to lead to the discovery of admissible evidence)

INITIATING WRITTEN DISCOVERY REQUESTS, cont.

(Interrogatories; Requests for Production; Requests for Admission)

Practical Tips:

Interrogatories (FRCP 33) (cont.)

- consult internal discovery plan (to make sure you are seeking all relevant information)
- good idea to use definitions and instructions (to narrowly tailor requests)
- determine whether your requests may be objectionable (if so, delete or alter)

Requests for Production (FRCP 34) (cont.)

- consult internal discovery plan (to make sure you are seeking all relevant information)
- good idea to use definitions and instructions (to narrowly tailor requests)
- determine whether your requests may be objectionable (if so, delete or alter)

Requests for Admission (FRCP 36) (cont.)

- consult internal discovery plan (to make sure you are seeking all relevant information)
- good idea to use definitions and instructions (to narrowly tailor requests)

*NOTE: According to FRCP 26(d), these forms of discovery may not be taken prior to the Parties' Planning Meeting under FRCP 26(f) (unless a local rule, order, or agreement states otherwise.)

RESPONDING TO WRITTEN DISCOVERY REQUESTS

(Interrogatories; Requests for Production; Requests for Admission)

General Tips for Responses

- must respond within 30 days (unless otherwise stipulated or ordered by court; *see FRCP 29 re: discovery stipulations*)

- with respect to each request, must either answer or object (or answer part and object to the rest) (*see FRCP 33(b)(4) requiring that objections to interrogatories be stated with specificity*)

- by signing answers and objections, an attorney is certifying under FRCP 26(g)(2) that they are are (A) consistent with these rules and warranted by existing law (or good faith argument for change), (B) not interposed for any improper purpose, and (C) not unreasonable or unduly burdensome or expensive (and sanctions may be imposed if these are violated)

- the party answering the interrogatories must sign them (in addition to their attorney)

Potential Objections

- **irrelevant** (and not reasonably calculated to lead to the discovery of admissible evidence) (*see FRCP 26(b)(1)*)

- **privileged** (*see FRCP 26(b)(1)*) (same as under rules of evidence—defined by constitutional provisions, statutory law, common law, rules of evidence and cases interpreting them)
  (e.g. attorney / client, doctor / patient, etc.)
  (**Note** FRCP 26(b)(5), requiring this objection to be made expressly)

- **work-product** (FRCP 26(b)(3)) (trial preparation materials) (qualified privilege, covering documents and tangible things prepared in anticipation of litigation or for trial—can only get if show substantial need and undue hardship)
  (**Note:** FRCP 26(b)(5) applies to this type of objection as well)

RESPONDING TO WRITTEN DISCOVERY REQUESTS, cont.
(Interrogatories; Requests for Production; Requests for Admission)

General Tips for Responses (cont.)

- *see FRCP 26(e)(2)* for a continuing duty to supplement discovery responses

- responses must be served on other side (*see FRCP 5*), and filed with the court (unless prohibited by local court rule)

- *see FRCP 33(d)* re: option to provide business records in lieu of answering certain interrogatories

- when responding to document requests, must both respond in writing and produce all relevant documents (*see FRCP 34(b)*)

- when producing documents in response to document request, must produce them as they are kept in the usual course of business or must organize them and label them to correspond with the categories in the request (*see FRCP 34(b)*)

Potential Objections (cont.)

- **experts** (*see FRCP 26(b)(4)*) (if non-testifying expert, can get no discovery unless show exceptional circumstances and pay reasonable fee)

- **annoying, embarrassing (confidential), oppressive, or undue burden or expense** (but must seek protective order— *see FRCP 26(c), 26(b)(2)*)

- **vague or ambiguous**

- **overbroad**

- **excessive detail or number**

- **(re: interrogatories...)**

  - seeks pure legal conclusions

  - seeks documents or verbatim contents only available under FRCP 34

MOTIONS FOR PHYSICAL / MENTAL EXAMINATIONS
(FRCP 35)

PURPOSE

Allows other side to have own doctor examine person whose condition is at issue— to help with defense or cross-examination

WHO CAN BE EXAMINED

- party

OR

- person in custody or under legal control of party

GROUNDS

- person's physical or mental condition is in controversy
- good cause exists (relevant, and info is needed—weighing pain, danger, intrusiveness against usefulness)

CONTENT OF MOTION

- grounds
- specify:
  - time
  - place
  - manner
  - conditions
  - scope

  of examination
- identify examiner (suitably licensed or certified)

  (or can stipulate to exam with other side)

(**Note:** If the examinee requests a copy of the report it must be provided to him, and such a request triggers the reciprocal exchange of all reports on such condition. *See FRCP 35(b)(1)*.)

TAKING / DEFENDING / USING DEPOSITIONS

Initiating Depo

- If deponent is party, serve Notice of Deposition (FRCP 30(b))

- If deponent is non-party, serve subpoena under FRCP 45 (see FRCP 30(a)(1))

(For instances where leave of court required, see FRCP 30(a)(2))

(See FRCP 30(b)(2), (3), (7) re: method by which testimony will be recorded)

Conduct During Depo*

- Opening statement on the record by court reporter (FRCP 30(b)(4))

- Deponent placed under oath (FRCP 30(c))

- Examination and Cross-Examination (see FRCP 30(c))

- Re: objections, see FRCP 30(c), (d); FRCP 32(d)

(Transcript reviewed by deponent or not; certified and filed by officer. See FRCP 30(e), (f))

Use of Depo at Trial

See FRCP 32

(See, also, FRCP 26(b)(4)(A) (re: Deposing Expert Witnesses); FRCP 27 (Depositions Before Action or Pending Appeal); FRCP 28 (Persons Before Whom Depositions May Be Taken); and FRCP 31 (Depositions Upon Written Questions).)

* If court assistance is needed, see chart entitled "Seeking Court Assistance in the Discovery Process."

SEEKING COURT ASSISTANCE IN THE DISCOVERY PROCESS*

Seeking Protection from Discovery

- Motion for Protective Order under FRCP 26(c) if claiming that discovery is annoying, embarrassing, oppressive, or requires undue burden or expense (*see numerous types of protection listed in rule*)

- Motion for Protective Order under FRCP 26(c) and 26(b)(2) if seeking some type of limitation on frequency or extent of use of discovery methods (*see the three bases for such limitations in FRCP 26(b)(2)*)

- *See, also, FRCP 30(d)(2), (3)* re: protection during depositions

Compelling Discovery

- FRCP 37(a) Motion for Order Compelling Disclosure or Discovery (and can get expenses of motion—(a)(4))

- FRCP 30(d)(2) Motion for Additional Deposition Time (if needed for fair examination or if deponent or another party impedes or delays examination)

(*When filing a FRCP 26(c) or FRCP 37 motion, the movant must certify that he first attempted to resolve the dispute with opposing counsel without court action.)

Seeking Discovery Sanctions

- FRCP 37(b) Motion for Sanctions for Failure to Comply with Court Order (under 37(a))

- FRCP 37(c) Motion for Sanctions re: Disclosures / Refusals to Make Admissions

- FRCP 37(d) Motion for Sanctions re: Party's Complete Failure to Participate / Respond

- FRCP 37(g) Motion for Sanctions re: Failure to Participate in Framing of Discovery Plan (under 26(f))

- FRCP 30(d)(2), (3) re: sanctions during a deposition

- FRCP 30(g) Motion for Expenses for Party's Failure to Attend Depo or Serve Subpoena on Witness

- FRCP 26(g) (Rule 11—equivalent for discovery) Motion for Sanctions for Incorrect / Incomplete Disclosures ((g)(1)) or Requests or Responses or Objections that Violate (g)(2)

Chapter 9

Pretrial Resolution of Cases

In addition to Pre-Answer motions and settlements, there are at least four ways to resolve a lawsuit prior to trial. See the chart entitled *Pretrial Resolution of Cases.*

The first possibility is a default judgment under FRCP 55. If a defendant fails to timely respond to a Complaint (under FRCP 12), a plaintiff may first seek an entry of default, by filing an affidavit with the clerk of court (under FRCP 55(a)), and then seek a default judgment (under FRCP 55(b)). Depending upon the circumstances, the default judgment can be obtained from either the clerk or the court. It can be obtained from the clerk, under FRCP 55(b)(1), if plaintiff's claim against defendant is for a sum certain or for a sum which can by computation be made certain. For example, this requirement may be met where there is a reasonable liquidated damages amount involved. There is no provision for notice of this action to the defendant. If the lawsuit does not fit within the parameters of FRCP 55(b)(1), the default judgment must be obtained from the judge (under FRCP 55(b)(2)). The plaintiff must file a motion for default judgment with the court, and the court, in its discretion, may hold a hearing. If the defendant has "appeared" in the action (by demonstrating a clear purpose to defend the lawsuit — other than by filing an Answer), defendant must be served with written notice of the motion at least three days prior to the hearing. (*Note:* A defendant must show "good cause" to set aside an entry of default under FRCP 55(c). If an actual default judgment has been entered, the defendant must file a motion to set aside the judgment under FRCP 60(b).)

Another way to resolve a lawsuit is for it to be voluntarily dismissed. A plaintiff can dismiss his or her own lawsuit as of right before the service of the Answer or a motion for summary judgment (whichever occurs first) under FRCP 41(a)(1)(i). The case can also be dismissed as of right through a stipulation of the parties (the usual way a settlement is effectuated) under FRCP 41(a)(1)(ii). (Note, however, that there are exceptions to these rules. The parties need court permission, even under these circumstances, if it is a settlement or dismissal of a class action under FRCP 23(e), if the case involves a receiver appointed by a federal court under FRCP 66, or as provided in any United States statute (e.g. an action brought on behalf of incompetents).) Other than these situations (and exceptions) under FRCP 41(a)(1), any dismissal by plaintiff of his or her suit must be by leave of court (upon such terms and conditions as the court deems proper). See FRCP 41(a)(2).

A third way to resolve a lawsuit prior to trial is by involuntary dismissal under FRCP 41(b). Under this rule, a plaintiff's case may be dismissed involuntarily (upon motion by defendant or the court itself) for failure to prosecute (not proceeding with "due diligence") or failure to comply with court orders or rules. If the case is dismissed under this rule, it is usually *with* prejudice, and is a final, appealable order.

Finally, another pretrial method of resolving a case is a motion for summary judgment (on part or all of the case) under FRCP 56. The requirements for obtaining a judgment under this rule are that there is no genuine issue as to any material fact, and the moving party is entitled to judgment as a matter of law. See FRCP 56(c).

See, also, checklist #18, entitled *Pretrial Motions Checklist.*

PRETRIAL RESOLUTION OF CASES

Default Judgments (FRCP 55)

If D fails to timely respond to complaint

(a) Seek an **entry of default*** FRCP 55(a)

(b) Seek a **default judgment*** FRCP 55(b)

• by clerk (55(b)(1)) if seeking a sum certain or sum which can by computation be made certain

OR

• (otherwise) by the judge (55(b)(2))

(Note: must give D 3 days' written notice of default judgment hearing if D has "appeared" in the action)

Voluntary Dismissals (FRCP 41(a))

P can voluntarily dismiss own case

(1) as of right before service of the Answer or Summary Judgment motion (whichever is first) (a)(1)(i)

OR

(2) by stipulation of the parties (a)(1)(ii)

Otherwise, must seek leave of court (41(a)(2), and court will only grant it upon such terms and conditions as it deems proper

(*See exceptions to 41(a)(1) though*)

Involuntary Dismissals (FRCP 41(b))

P's case may be dismissed by court on two grounds:

(1) failure to prosecute (P must proceed to trial with "due diligence")

OR

(2) failure to comply with court orders or rules

(**Note:** If case is dismissed under either ground, it is usually with prejudice, and is a final, appealable order.)

Summary Judgment (FRCP 56)

May get judgment without trial if:

(1) no genuine issue as to any material fact

AND

(2) moving party entitled to judgment as a matter of law (*see 56(c)*)

[**To set aside entry of default, see FRCP 55(c); to set aside default judgment, see FRCP 60(b)*]

Chapter 10

Dispute Resolution Alternatives

At some point in every lawsuit, the court or counsel should consider whether the dispute can be resolved through some dispute resolution mechanism other than trial. See the chart entitled *Dispute Resolution Alternatives*. There is a continuum of ways that disputes are resolved — ranging from avoidance (doing nothing to resolve it) to litigation. In between are a number of mechanisms often lumped together under the term "alternative dispute resolution" or "ADR." Included within this group are the following methods (and brief definitions thereof):

—*Negotiation* — communication back and forth between people who have a dispute and are trying to resolve it.

—*Conciliation* — the use of a third person to bring the parties together and then leave them to resolve their own dispute.

—*Mediation* — the use of a third person, with no power to make a decision, who tries to help the parties resolve their own dispute (facilitated negotiation).

Some hybrid dispute resolution processes (and a brief definition thereof) include:

—*Variants of Arbitration*

—*Court-annexed (non-binding) arbitration* — an informal hearing with one or three arbitrators who listen to testimony and then reach a non-binding decision (that the court hopes will be the basis for a settlement of that pending case).

—*Med-Arb* — a process that the parties agree will begin as a mediation and then, if it does not result in settlement, will proceed to arbitration.

—*Mini-Trial* — a summarized presentation of the case by attorneys (usually in a complex case involving corporate parties) to a panel consisting of the chief executive officers of both parties plus a neutral person, followed by settlement discussions.

—*Summary Jury Trial* — a summarized presentation by attorneys to a real jury, who then deliberates and reaches a nonbinding verdict, upon which settlement discussions are based.

—*Neutral Expert Fact-Finding* — the use of a neutral person to find facts in a case to aid a negotiation, mediation or adjudication.

—*Early Neutral Evaluation (E.N.E.)* — the use of a neutral person to assess the relative strengths and weaknesses of the parties' cases and the probable outcome, to help identify issues, to help the parties identify areas of agreement and enter into stipulations, to help the parties agree on a discovery plan, etc.

—*Private Judging* — a process available under some statutes or court rules where a privately selected and paid neutral party decides the case and then the decision is entered as a judgment of the court.

—*Ombudsmen/Ombudspersons* — the use of an official appointed by an institution to investigate complaints and either prevent disputes or facilitate their resolution within that institution.

—*Settlement Conferences/Settlement Facilitation* — the use of a conference with a judge or other neutral person to attempt to convince or assist the parties to settle.

The remaining methods on the chart consist of various forms of adjudication. They include court trials; voluntary, private, binding arbitration; and administrative hearings.

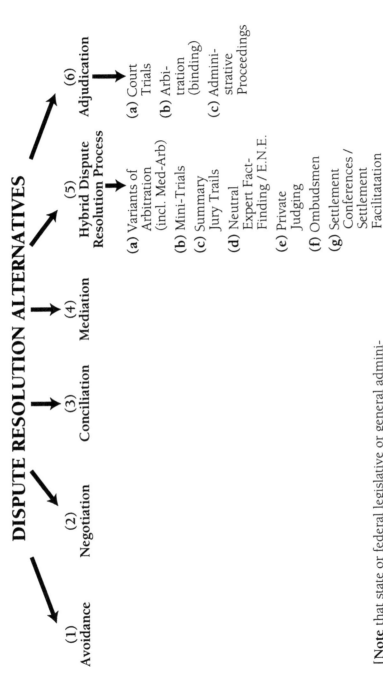

DISPUTE RESOLUTION ALTERNATIVES

(1)
Avoidance

(2)
Negotiation

(3)
Conciliation

(4)
Mediation

(5)
Hybrid Dispute
Resolution Process

(a) Variants of
Arbitration
(incl. Med-Arb)

(b) Mini-Trials

(c) Summary
Jury Trails

(d) Neutral
Expert Fact-
Finding / E.N.E.

(e) Private
Judging

(f) Ombudsmen

(g) Settlement
Conferences /
Settlement
Facilitatation

(6)
Adjudication

(a) Court
Trials

(b) Arbi-
tration
(binding)

(c) Admini-
strative
Proceedings

[**Note** that state or federal legislative or general administrative processes can be used to resolve disputes as well.]

Chapter 11

Components of Settlements

If, at any time during the pendency of the lawsuit, the case is settled, the parties should enter into a written settlement agreement and should file a court order disposing of the case. See the chart entitled *Components of Settlements*.

Like any contract, a written settlement agreement should adequately express the intentions of the parties. Among the provisions that should be included are: the names of the parties; mention of the pending lawsuit (including the case number); consideration and mutual releases of all pending or future related claims; a clear statement of what each party is to do under the agreement (e.g. with respect to the payment of funds and the filing of the stipulation of dismissal); a confidentiality clause (if desired); a denial of liability provision; a provision stating that this constitutes the entire agreement of the parties (to avoid parole evidence problems); and a description of how the case will be disposed of and who will pay the costs of suit.

The court order disposing of the case will generally be a Stipulated Notice of Dismissal under FRCP 41(a)(1)(ii),(c). It is important that such an order specifically state which party will pay the court costs (or whether each side will pay their own), and that dismissal of claims will be *with* prejudice (so that they cannot be filed again).

(*Note to defense counsel:* See FRCP 68 for the advantages of putting a settlement offer in the form of an Offer of Judgment under that rule. Briefly stated, if the case does not settle and the Offer of Judgment exceeded the plaintiff's recovery at trial, defendant will not have to pay plaintiff's post-offer costs and plaintiff will have to pay defendant's post-offer costs.)

See, also, checklists #20 and #21, entitled *Settlement Agreement Checklist*, and *Court Document Disposing of Settled Case Checklist*.

COMPONENTS OF SETTLEMENTS

Written Agreement

- In contract format
- Include names of parties
- Mention pending suit
- Include consideration / mutual releases of all pending or future related claims
- Specify what each party is to do (e.g. payment of funds—when? how? in what form? / filing of stipulation of dismissal —who will do it? when? in what form?)
- Include confidentiality provision (if desired)
- Include denial of liability provision
- Include provision re: this constituting entire agreement of the parties
- Mention disposition of suit / payment of costs

Court Order Disposing of Case

- Stipulated voluntary dismissal (e.g. FRCP 41(a)(1)(ii), (c)) (or consent judgment)
- Mention payment of costs (e.g. each side to pay own)
- Specify effect of dismissal (e.g. *all* claims dismissed *with* prejudice)

(Note to defendants: See FRCP 68 for the advantages of putting a settlement offer in the form of an Offer of Judgment under that rule.)

Chapter 12

Seeking Appellate Review Prior to Final Judgment

The general rule is that only final judgments can be appealed. See 28 U.S.C. section 1291. However, there are at least five possible ways to seek appellate review of a trial court decision prior to final judgment.* See the chart entitled *Seeking Appellate Review Prior to Final Judgment*.

The *first* method is under FRCP 54(b). This rule applies when a case has multiple claims and/or multiple parties and the judge makes a decision as to one or more of the claims or parties before the rest are decided (e.g. by granting a motion for summary judgment as to that claim or party). If the trial court agrees to make a FRCP 54(b) certification as to that part of the case, the ruling may be appealed immediately. To comply with FRCP 54(b), a trial court must direct the entry of a final judgment as to that one claim or party upon an express determination that there is no just reason for delay and upon an express direction for the entry of judgment. However, it is within the trial court's discretion as to whether a FRCP 54(b) certification will be made, and if the trial court declines to make one, the parties must wait to appeal until the entire case has been decided. If a FRCP 54(b) certification is made, that part of the case is considered "final" within the terms of the final judgment rule (28 U.S.C. section 1291), and so the appellate court must hear the appeal.

The *second* way to appeal prior to final judgment is through 28 U.S.C. section 1292(a). This statutory provision makes appealable (among other things) interlocutory orders concerning *injunctions* (including those granting, continuing, modifying, refusing or dissolving injunctions, or refusing to dissolve or modify injunctions). This exception to the final judgment rule is based upon the fact that

73

injunctions are rather drastic measures and can cause harm that sometimes cannot be undone. Therefore, immediate review of such orders is warranted.

The *third* method for obtaining review of interlocutory trial court decisions is through 28 U.S.C. section 1292(b). This is a discretionary standard for interlocutory appeals and applies when the trial court judge is of the opinion that (1) a particular interlocutory order involves a controlling question of law as to which there is substantial ground for difference of opinion and (2) an immediate appeal from the order may materially advance the ultimate termination of the litigation. If the district court, within its discretion, decides that these two requirements have been met, he "certifies" it for interlocutory appeal (and must state so in writing in the order). Then, within ten days of the order, the appealing party must apply to the appellate court to take the appeal. The appellate court also has the discretion to decide whether or not to allow the appeal.

The *fourth* way to appeal prior to final judgment is through the *collateral order doctrine* under *Cohen v. Beneficial Industrial Loan Corp.*, 337 U.S. 541 (1949). Like FRCP 54(b), if the doctrine is applicable, the decision is considered "final" under 28 U.S.C. section 1291 and the appellate court must hear it. An (otherwise interlocutory) order falls within the *Cohen* exception (and so can be appealed prior to the end of the case) if it satisfies at least three conditions. It must: (1) conclusively determine the disputed question (finality); (2) resolve an important issue completely separate from the merits of the action (collateral); and (3) be effectively unreviewable on appeal from a final judgment. If these conditions are met, it can be appealed immediately (even though portions of the case are undecided). This doctrine allows the appellate court to offer guidance on important issues that otherwise might not be reviewed without concern that it will result in duplicative consideration through piece-meal appeals.

The *fifth* way to seek appellate review of an interlocutory trial court order or decision is a petition for writ of mandamus. This technically is not an appeal, but is, instead, an independent proceeding filed in the appellate court against a public official (generally the judge or the court) to require him to do his duty. It is extraordinary because it is not supposed to be a substitute for an appeal and is therefore only available when there is no other adequate means to achieve the desired remedy and where there is present an abuse of judicial power.

(*See, also, the very recent amendment to FRCP 23 (the class action rule). Effective December 1, 1998, FRCP 23 was amended by adding a new subdivision (f) to provide the courts of appeals with discretion to hear interlocutory appeals from orders granting or denying class certification.)

SEEKING APPELLATE REVIEW PRIOR TO FINAL JUDGMENT

FRCP 54(b)	28 U.S.C. 1292(a)	28 U.S.C. 1292(b)	Collateral Order	Writ of Mandamus
Where case has **multiple claims or parties** and court makes decision as to one of them	All interlocutory orders re: **injunctions** can be appealed immediately	If court certifies that interlocutory order involves **controlling question of law** as to which there is **substantial ground for difference of opinion** and that **immediate appeal from the order may materially advance the ultimate termination of the litigation**, can appeal immediately	An interlocutory order may be appealed immediately (and considered "final" under 28 U.S.C. 1291) **if:**	(Technically not an appeal, since it is a new case filed in appellate court)
Can appeal that decision **if** (in court's discretion) court directs entry of a final judgment as to that party or claim and expressly determines no just reason for delay and expressly directs entry of judgment	(including orders granting, continuing, modifying, refusing or dissolving injunctions or refusing to dissolve or modify injunctions)	(but both trial court and appellate court have discretion)	(1) it conclusively determines the disputed question;	Extraordinary remedy to force judge or other public official to do his duty
(if so, becomes "final" under 28 U.S.C. 1291)	(applies to preliminary injunctions, not TROs)		(2) it resolves an important issue completely separate from the merits of the action, and	Only available when no other adequate means to attain the desired relief / abuse of power
			(3) it would be effectively unreviewable on appeal from a final judgment	

(*See, also,* FRCP 23(*f*), effective 12/1/98 re: discretionary interlocutory appeals from class action certification orders)

Chapter 13

Preparing for Trial

Depending upon which court the case is in, and which judge is deciding it, there are at least five possible tasks you may need to perform to prepare for trial. See the chart entitled *Preparing for Trial*.

The first task is to file all possible pretrial motions. These might include FRCP 56 summary judgment motions (on all or part of the case), motions in limine (under the Federal Rules of Evidence) to get advance evidentiary rulings about trial testimony or exhibits, FRCP 42(a) motions to consolidate cases for trial, and motions to have separate trials on certain claims or issues (under FRCP 21 or 42(b)).

An additional task required by a number of judges is to prepare an individual or joint pretrial statement. Most commonly this includes categories such as stipulated facts, issues of fact to be tried, issues of law to be tried, a list of expert and lay witnesses who will testify at the trial, and a list of trial exhibits. (Sometimes proposed jury instructions will be submitted as part of the pretrial statement.)

Many cases will include a final pretrial conference, under FRCP 16(d), at which time any remaining pretrial issues will be resolved. If a joint pretrial statement has been submitted, often it will be adopted by the court in form of a final pretrial order under FRCP 16(e). This order will control the course of the trial, and no modifications can be made to it except to prevent manifest injustice. See FRCP 16(e).

In all jury trial cases, attorneys have the right to — and should — submit proposed jury instructions to the judge. See FRCP 51. Under FRCP 51, the judge must then inform counsel prior to closing arguments what jury instructions will be given to the jury. Any objections to such instructions should be made at that time, in order to preserve the issue for appeal.

Finally, some courts require counsel to submit trial briefs on the relevant legal issues in the case. The timing and requirements for such briefs vary from judge to judge.

Note, also, the automatic disclosure requirements re: the identity of, and reports from, expert witnesses who will testify, under FRCP 26(a)(2), and the automatic disclosure requirements re: the identification of other trial witnesses and trial exhibits, under FRCP 26(a)(3).

See, also, checklists #18 and #19, entitled *Pretrial Motions Checklist*, and *Joint Pretrial Statement Checklist*.

PREPARING FOR TRIAL

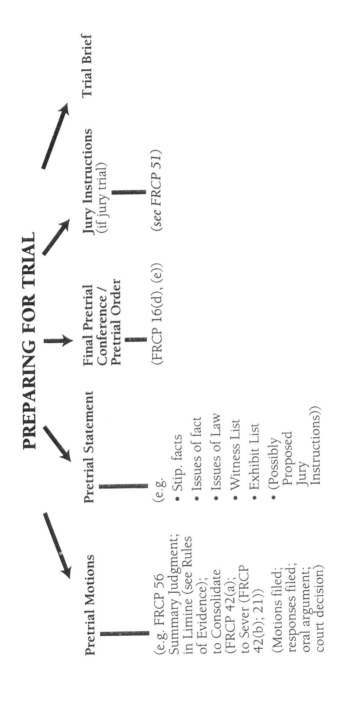

Pretrial Motions

(e.g. FRCP 56
Summary Judgment;
in Limine (see Rules
of Evidence);
to Consolidate
(FRCP 42(a);
to Sever (FRCP
42(b); 21))

(Motions filed;
responses filed;
oral argument;
court decision)

Pretrial Statement

(e.g.
• Stip. facts
• Issues of fact
• Issues of Law
• Witness List
• Exhibit List

• (Possibly
  Proposed
  Jury
  Instructions))

**Final Pretrial
Conference /
Pretrial Order**

(FRCP 16(d), (e))

Jury Instructions
(if jury trial)

(see FRCP 51)

Trial Brief

(*See, also,* the automatic disclosure requirements re: the identity of,
and reports from, expert witnesses who will testify, under FRCP 26(a)(2),
and the automatic disclosure requirements re: the identification of other
trial witnesses and trial exhibits, under FRCP 26(a)(3).)

Chapter 14

Basic Jury Trial Stages

There are a number of common stages in the average jury trial. See the chart entitled *Basic Jury Trial Stages*. The point of the chart is to demonstrate at what points during the basic jury trial that the burden of production issue is raised by either party (potentially allowing for the immediate entry of a judgment). The trial process begins, of course, after the jurors have been selected through the *voir dire* process (see 28 U.S.C. sections 1861-1871, and FRCP 47 and 48).

The trial generally starts with opening statements by both sides (although the defense can delay their opening statement until they put on their evidence). The plaintiff then puts on its case through the presentation of evidence in the form of testimony and exhibits. The defense may cross-examine plaintiff's witnesses. At the close of plaintiff's case, the defendant may make a motion for judgment as a matter of law (JML) (formerly called directed verdict), under FRCP 50. (*Note:* The plaintiff cannot make a JML motion at this point, even if it thinks that based upon its evidence no rational jury could find in favor of the defendant. This is based upon the ground that due process of law entitles every litigant to an opportunity to be heard before a court adjudicates his rights. If the court could grant a judgment as a matter of law for the plaintiff at the close of his own case, then the defendant would be deprived of his opportunity to present evidence, either to refute the plaintiff's case or to establish an affirmative defense. Even if the judge concludes that the plaintiff's evidence would support a JML in its favor, the defendant may well produce countervailing evidence that would leave legitimate doubt as to the facts, making the case an appropriate one for the jury. Therefore, no matter how strong the plaintiff's evidence may be, the defendant will be given a chance to rebut it.)

Assuming that the court denies the defendant's initial JML motion (as is most often the case), the defendant will then put on its evidence, again through testimony and exhibits. (Note that it is possible that the plaintiff will be allowed to put on rebuttal evidence after the defendant's case, and that the defendant may put on rebuttal evidence after the plaintiff has done so.) After both parties have rested, either party may make a JML motion. (*Note* that while the two points mentioned above are the traditional times at which the JML motion is made, FRCP 50 makes it clear that such a motion can be made at any time after a party has been fully heard with respect to an *issue* (and the motion is directed to that issue).)

If the JML motions are denied, both parties make their closing arguments, the judge instructs the jury (see FRCP 51), the jury deliberates and renders a verdict (see FRCP 48, 49), and the judge enters a judgment on the verdict (see FRCP 58).

Within ten days after the entry of the judgment, the losing party may make a renewed motion for judgment as a matter of law (RJML) (formerly called a motion for judgment notwithstanding the verdict, or JNOV) (50(b)) or, in the alternative, a motion for new trial (59). (Note that FRCP 50(a)(2) makes it clear that a JML motion during trial is a prerequisite for a RJML motion. The Advisory Committee Notes state that the purpose of this requirement is to give the responding party an opportunity to cure any deficiency in that party's proof that may have been overlooked until called to the party's attention by a late motion for judgment.)

Within thirty days of the entry of judgment or the resolution of the above-mentioned post-trial motions, the losing party may appeal.

The final stage of a lawsuit is the execution of the judgment (see FRCP 69).

BASIC JURY TRIAL STAGES
(showing when the burden of production issue is raised)

(After the jurors are selected through the *voir dire* process
(see 28 U.S.C. sections 1861-1871, and FRCP 47 and 48))

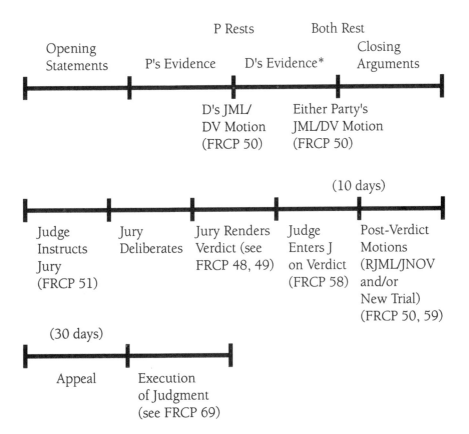

*Note that it is possible that P will put on rebuttal evidence
after D's case, and that D may then put on rebuttal evidence
after P's rebuttal evidence.

Chapter 15

Post-Trial Motions

The two main types of post-trial motions are motions for new trial, under FRCP 59, and renewed motions for judgment as a matter of law (formerly called motions for judgment notwithstanding the verdict, or JNOV), under FRCP 50. Both motions must be filed within *ten days* after the entry of the judgment, and they can be filed at the same time (in the alternative). The timing and interrelationship between the rulings on these motions are demonstrated by the chart entitled *Renewed Motions for Judgment as a Matter of Law (RJML) (Formerly JNOV)/Motions for New Trial*. A second chart lists the possible grounds for a new trial motion.

The assumption underlying the first chart is that the plaintiff has won a jury verdict, and that, within ten days after the judgment is entered, the defendant files either a renewed motion for judgment as a matter of law (RJML) (FRCP 50(b)) or a motion for new trial (FRCP 59) or both.

If the defendant has filed *only* a RJML (under FRCP 50(b)) (formerly called a motion for judgment notwithstanding the verdict, or JNOV), the court's options depend upon whether the RJML is warranted. If the RJML is warranted, the court has *two choices*. The *first choice* is that the court can *grant* the RJML in the defendant's favor. (This is a final judgment, so the plaintiff can file an appeal or can move for a new trial instead, within ten days, under FRCP 50(c)(2).) The court's *second choice* is that it can, in its discretion, order a new trial instead within ten days after the judgment is entered, under FRCP 50(b), 59(d). (The court possibly can do so even after the ten-day period *if* a RJML is warranted, on the theory that such a remedy cannot possibly prejudice the plaintiff. Obviously it is better for the plaintiff to have to try the case again than it is to lose altogether.) With this second option it does not matter if a motion for new trial was made. The court's discretion should be guided largely by an estimate of the likelihood that the party who received the defective verdict may be able to fill in the gaps in a second trial. This decision (to grant a new trial) is not a final judgment, since a new trial will take place.

On the other hand, if the RJML is *not* warranted, the court also has *two choices. First*, it can deny the RJML, which is a final judgment (allowing the defendant to appeal). *Second*, it can grant a new trial instead. (But the court cannot grant a new trial unless a timely motion for new trial was made *or* the court orders a new trial on its own initiative *"not later than 10 days after the entry of judgment"* (Rule 59(d)). This situation is different than that discussed in the paragraph above because this *is* prejudicial to the plaintiff because the RJML for the defendant is not warranted and thus the original verdict should stand.) This is not a final judgment, since a new trial will take place.

If the defendant files *both* a RJML motion and a new trial motion at the same time (in the alternative), which is fairly typical, the court is required to rule on both motions (FRCP 50(c)). There are *three* principal variations involved in this situation. *First*, if the trial court *denies both motions*, the original judgment can be appealed by the defendant (since it is final), and the rulings on the post-trial motions are reviewed therein. (If the trial court denied both motions, the *appellate court* will affirm the original judgment if it concludes that the motions were properly denied. If the appellate court finds that the original judgment should be *reversed*, it has *three options*: (1) it can direct entry of a RJML (if it further determines that a new trial is inappropriate), (2) it can order a new trial, or (3) it can remand to the trial court to make the new trial determination (or for a reconsideration of the motion for new trial).)

Second, if the trial court *denies the motion for RJML, but grants the motion for new trial*, there will be a new trial (and, thus, no appeal since it is not a final judgment). (And the question of the validity of the new trial order can only be raised on the plaintiff's appeal of the eventual final judgment after the *second* trial. The question of whether the RJML motion should have been granted ordinarily thereby becomes moot. Note that it is difficult to show that even if the denial of the RJML motion were erroneous, it had a prejudicial effect in the second trial.)

Third, if the trial court *grants the motion for RJML, its conditional ruling* (specifically required by FRCP 50(c)(1)) *on the new trial motion* (whether it is granted or denied) is basically an *advisory indication to the appellate court* as to what decision that court might make if it reverses the RJML decision. (Since granting a RJML ends the case and is a final judgment, FRCP 50(c)(1) requires that a conditional ruling be made on the new trial motion in the event that the appellate court reverses the RJML.) This is a final judgment so the plaintiff can appeal (or can move for a new trial instead, within ten days, under FRCP 50(c)(2)). Since the trial court granted the RJML, the appellate court can affirm it if it decides that the motion was properly granted. If the *appellate court* decides that the RJML was improper (and thus reverses), again, it has *three choices*: (a) it can order reentry of the original judgment; (2) it can grant a new trial (being strongly guided, but not bound, by the trial court's *conditional ruling* on an alternative new trial motion), or (3) it can remand to the trial court for reconsideration of the motion for new trial.

Finally, it should be made clear that a proper motion for judgment as a matter of law (JML) (formerly called a motion for directed verdict) is a prerequisite for a RJML motion.

Since the new trial motions rule (FRCP 59) does not itself delineate the possible grounds for new trial, see the additional chart in this chapter, entitled *Grounds for New Trial Motions*. Under common law, most grounds for new trial fall into one of two categories: *(1)* errors in the *trial process* (including errors in the law applied) — or the procedure leading up to the verdict, and *(2)* errors in the *jury's evaluation of the evidence* — or the correctness of the verdict itself. See *Civil Procedure* (4th ed.), by Stephen C. Yeazell (Little, Brown & Company, 1996), at pp. 732-741. A third category — post-trial problems — exists as well.

The *first* category of errors (those in the trial process itself) include *judicial errors* in instructing the jury (e.g. by giving them an incorrect statement of the law), admitting evidence, and commenting on the evidence (e.g. by, in effect, directing a verdict). This category also includes *misconduct* by parties (e.g. by approaching a juror to tell or give him something — like a bribe), counsel (e.g. exceeding the bounds of proper closing argument), witnesses (e.g. by volunteering a statement that the defendant is insured — a fact that normally is inadmissible), and jurors (e.g. by conducting an improper outside experiment). In addition, a *prejudicial happenstance* during the trial can lead to the granting of a new trial motion. An example of this latter category is the presence of a blind man sitting in the courtroom very close to the plaintiff, in a case where there has been an injury to his eye.

The judge has the *discretion* to grant a new trial under any of the above circumstances, but he or she will not do so if the error is deemed harmless. (See FRCP 61.) No verdict may be set aside and a new trial granted unless the error adversely affected the substantial rights of the losing party. The trial judge is given such discretion because of his or her superior ability to assess the prejudicial effect of errors on the trial process. (Note that the standard of review on appeal of a decision on a new trial motion is *abuse of discretion*.)

With respect to the *second* category of grounds for new trials — problems with the verdict itself — there are three general bases. The first is *inconsistent verdicts*, in the context of special verdicts and general verdicts with interrogatories. Unlike general verdicts, these unusual verdict forms pose potential consistency problems which, if they cannot be remedied, can only be cured by a new trial. *FRCP 49(a)* authorizes a *special verdict* in which the court submits only a list of factual issues to the jury and requests it to make findings. The judge then applies the law to these findings to enter the appropriate judgment. If the answers to these issues are not consistent with each other (and cannot be harmonized or reconsidered in order to cure the inconsistency), a new trial should be ordered. *FRCP 49(b)* authorizes a general verdict accompanied by answers to written interrogatories. With this verdict form the judge instructs the jury to reach a general verdict, but also requests answers to one or more questions so that the basis for that verdict is disclosed. If the answers to the questions are consistent among themselves, but one or more is inconsistent with the general verdict, then the judge may order a new trial, or return both to the jury for further deliberation, or disregard the general verdict and enter judgment in accordance with the specific answers. If the answers are inconsistent with each other and one or more is also inconsistent with the general verdict, the judge either must request further deliberation by the jury or order a new trial.

Another ground for new trial in this second category is that the *verdict is against the weight of the evidence*. The judge should grant a new trial if he or she is of the opinion that the verdict is against the clear weight of the evidence, even though there may be substantial evidence which would prevent the granting of a renewed motion for judgment as a matter of law. Another formulation of this standard is that the trial court should not interfere with the verdict unless it is quite clear that the jury has reached a seriously erroneous result, and thus that it should not set the verdict aside merely because the court would have come to a different conclusion had it been the trier of the facts. See *Lind v. Schenley Industries, Inc.*, 278 F.2d 79, 89 (3rd Cir. 1960).

A third ground for new trial in this second category is *excessive and insufficient damages: remittitur and additur*. When the problem or error in the first trial involves the size of the verdict, a court may either order a new trial limited to the issue of damages or order a conditional new trial (conditioned on the acceptance of remittitur). (While additur — the power to increase damages — is not allowed in federal courts, a number of state courts allow it.) In the latter situation, the judge can state that he or she will grant the new trial motion unless the opposing party agrees to accept a specified reduction in the verdict.

The *third* category — post-trial problems — primarily involves motions for new trial on the ground of newly discovered evidence. Note, however, that if such evidence is found more than ten days after the entry of the judgment, a motion to set aside the judgment would have to be filed under FRCP 60(b)(2).

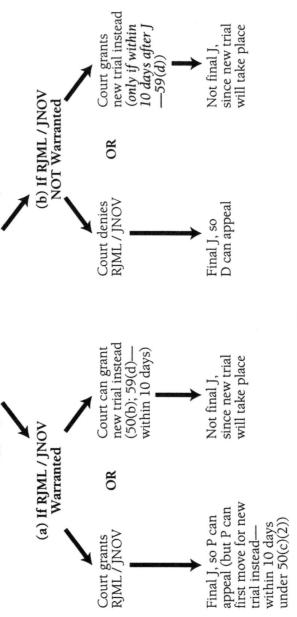

RENEWED MOTIONS FOR JUDGMENT AS A MATTER OF LAW (RJML) (FORMERLY JNOV) / MOTIONS FOR NEW TRIAL

P wins a jury verdict; within 10 days after the judgment is entered, D files either:

(1) 50(b) RENEWED MOTION FOR JUDGMENT AS A MATTER OF LAW (RJML) (JNOV) ONLY
(same test as for ordering judgment as a matter of law (JML) (formerly directed verdict))

(a) If RJML / JNOV Warranted

OR

Court grants RJML / JNOV

Final J, so P can appeal (but P can first move for new trial instead— within 10 days under 50(c)(2))

Court can grant new trial instead (50(b); 59(d)— within 10 days)

Not final J, since new trial will take place

(b) If RJML / JNOV NOT Warranted

Court denies RJML / JNOV

Final J, so D can appeal

OR

Court grants new trial instead (only if within 10 days after J —59(d))

Not final J, since new trial will take place

OR

RENEWED MOTIONS FOR JUDGMENT AS A MATTER OF LAW (RJML) (FORMERLY JNOV) / MOTIONS FOR NEW TRIAL, cont.

(2) 50(b) RJML / JNOV MOTION, OR, IN THE ALTERNATIVE, 59 NEW TRIAL MOTION
(trial court must rule on *both* motions)

(a) Court denies *both* motions

→ Final J; D can appeal original J *and* post-trial motion rulings

→ *Appellate court* can *affirm* or... if appellate court finds original J should be reversed

→ direct entry of RJML / JNOV **OR** order new trial

(b) Court *denies* RJML / JNOV motion, but *grants* new trial motion

→ Not final J, since new trial will take place

(P can appeal new trial ruling *after* final J entered in second trial)

(RJML / JNOV ruling ordinarily moot)

→ *Appellate court* can *affirm* or... if appellate court finds original J should be reversed

→ remand to trial court for reconsideration of motion for new trial

(c) Court *grants* RJML / JNOV motion, (and *conditionally rules* on new trial motion— 50(c)(1) (whether grant or deny))

→ Final J; P can appeal (or P can move for new trial instead, 50(c)(2))

→ *Appellate court* can *affirm* or... if reverses RJML / JNOV, appellate court can:

→ order reentry of original J **OR** grant new trial **OR** remand to trial court for reconsideration of motion for new trial

(Note: a proper motion for judgment as a matter of law / directed verdict is a prerequisite for a reviewd motion for judgment as a matter of law / JNOV.)

GROUNDS FOR NEW TRIAL MOTIONS
(see FRCP 59)

I. ERRORS IN THE TRIAL PROCESS
A. Judicial Errors in
- instructing the jury
- admitting evidence
- commenting on the evidence

B. Misconduct by
- parties
- counsel
- witnesses
- jurors

C. Prejudicial Happenstance

II. ERRORS IN JURY'S EVALUATION OF EVIDENCE
A. Inconsistent Verdicts
(with special verdict forms)

1. Special Verdicts (FRCP 49(a))

2. General Verdicts with Interrogatories (FRCP 49(b))

B. Verdicts Against the Weight of the Evidence

C. Excessive and Insufficient Damages: Remittitur and Additur

III. POST-TRIAL PROBLEMS
(e.g. newly discovered evidence—if discovered within 10 days after trial; otherwise must move under FRCP 60(b)(2))

(*Note:* The harmles error rule applies to all new trial motions. *See FRCP 61.*)

Chapter 16

Appeals

There are three important issues with respect to appeals:(1) who may seek review?, (2) when may a decision be reviewed?, and(3) what is the scope of review? See the chart entitled *Appeals*. See, also, *Civil Procedure* (4th ed.), by Stephen C. Yeazell (Little, Brown & Company, 1996), at pp. 743-781.

The only persons who may seek review are *parties* who have been *adversely affected* and who *raised the issue below*. In general, the purpose of appeals is to correct improper decisions by lower courts when it is necessary to protect the losing party. First, you must be an actual party to the case in order to appeal. Second, you must have been adversely affected by the judgment. Obviously the party who loses the entire case may appeal. But what if they win part of the case? This "adversely affected" requirement means that if a party obtains relief on one claim or theory but not under another claim or theory (and the relief sought was identical under both), they cannot appeal (since ultimately they were not adversely affected). However, they can appeal if the rejected claim or theory would have entitled them to more or different relief (a *different judgment*). With respect to the third aspect of this issue, the general rule is that a party cannot raise an issue on appeal unless they objected to it during the trial proceedings. If no objection was made, the issue is waived. (The "plain error" rule is an exception to this doctrine and has been applied in certain situations where the error has seriously affected the fairness, integrity, or public reputation of judicial proceedings.)

The second issue is when a decision may be reviewed on appeal. The general rule is that under 28 U.S.C. section 1291, appeals lie only from "final decisions" of the district courts. (This is referred to as the "final judgment" rule.) For the circumstances under which appellate review can be sought prior to final judgment, see Chapter 12 on "Seeking Appellate Review Prior to Final Judgment." Once a judgment is set forth on a separate document (as required by FRCP 58), a Notice of Appeal must be filed within 30 days (under Federal Rule of Appellate Procedure 4(a)) or the appellate court will not have jurisdiction. (Note that if post-trial motions, such as a renewed motion for judgment as a matter of law or a motion for new trial, were filed, the thirty-day appeal time is temporarily suspended until the motions have been decided.)

The third issue is what scope of review the appellate court will use for particular issues in a case. The scope and standard of review that will be used by an appellate court will depend upon (1) the nature of the alleged error — whether it involved an issue of *fact* or one of *law*, or whether it was a *discretionary* decision; and(2) whether the trial was before a *jury* or a *judge*. The fullest scope of review is for alleged errors involving *questions of law* (e.g. an erroneous jury instruction, the admission of evidence, conclusions of law in a bench trial, 12(b)(6) motions, summary judgment motions, judgments as a matter of law or renewed judgments as a matter of law, etc.). These are decided on a *de novo* basis (meaning "anew") — under which the appellate court can freely substitute its judgment for that of the trial court. (The courts are divided about how to treat *mixed* questions of fact and law, e.g. negligence.) Remember, though, that the harmless error rule applies to all appeals. See 28 U.S.C. section 2111. Rulings that are committed to the trial court's *discretion* are reviewed under an *abuse of discretion* standard, which allows reversal only if the trial judge was clearly wrong. Some examples of these include rulings on motions for new trial, discovery orders, Rule 60(b) motions, and motions to transfer under 28 U.S.C. section 1404. *Findings of fact* receive greater deference than issues of law. In a case tried to a *judge* (a bench trial), a finding of fact may be overturned only if it is clearly erroneous (under FRCP 52(a)). It is a narrow scope of review, since there is a presumption that the judge's findings are correct, and it is quite similar to the abuse of discretion standard. When a *jury* trial is involved, the court will give even greater deference to the factual findings. If the appeal challenges the sufficiency of the evidence to support the judgment, the standard is the same as the trial judge uses to decide motions for judgment as a matter of law (or renewed motions for judgment as a matter of law) — whether a rational jury could have reached that verdict.

Finally, as mentioned above, the harmless error rule (28 U.S.C. section 2111) applies to all appeals. Therefore, alleged errors must have been harmful to the appellant in the sense that they have materially contributed to the adverse part of the judgment. The statute itself states that the appellate court is to disregard errors or defects "which do not affect the substantial rights of the parties."

APPEALS

Who May Seek Review

- a party to the suit
- who is adversely affected by the judgment
- who raised the issue below (with some exceptions)

When May A Decision Be Reviewed

- in general, appeals lie only from "final decisions" of district courts *(see the final judgment rule, 28 U.S.C. 1291)*

    (For exceptions, see chart on "Appealing Decisions Prior to Final Judgment")

- once *"judgment"* is set forth on a separate document (see FRCP 58), must appeal within *30 days* (or appellate court does not have jurisdiction) (F.R.App.P. 4(a))

    (Note: if post-trial motions were filed, this temporarily suspends the running of the 30-day period)

SCOPE OF REVIEW

Questions of Law

De novo standard (full review / anew)

(Ex.—erroneous jury instruction; error in admitting evidence, etc.)

Discretionary Decisions

Abuse of Discretion

(Ex.—new trial motions, discovery orders, 60(b) motions

Findings of Fact

Clearly erroneous (if bench trial) (FRCP 52(a));

whether rational jury could have reached verdict (if jury trial)

(Note: The harmles error rule applies to all appeals— *See 28 U.S.C. 2111.)*

Chapter 17

Review by the
U.S. Supreme Court

The U.S. Supreme Court provides the final opportunity for review of a federal court case. The Court has two types of jurisdiction — original and appellate. See the chart entitled *Review by the U.S. Supreme Court*. Original jurisdiction means that the Court handles the entire case; it begins and ends there. The Court has original and exclusive jurisdiction (meaning the case *must* be filed there) of all controversies between two or more states (under 28 U.S.C. section 1251(a)). It has original, but *not* exclusive, jurisdiction of cases involving ambassadors (and other public ministers, consuls, or vice consuls of foreign states), between the United States and a state, and by a state against the citizens of another state or against aliens (under 28 U.S.C. section 1251(b)).

Other than this small class of cases, the Court's jurisdiction is appellate (and is described in 28 U.S.C. sections 1253, 1254, 1257, and 1258). In 1988, Congress passed the "Supreme Court Case Selections Act" (Public Law 100-352), the main purpose of which was to eliminate virtually all of the remaining "appeal" bases for review by the Court and require cases to use the (discretionary) "certiorari" route. So, in general, this legislation eliminated all of the mandatory jurisdiction (review of decisions by "appeal") of the U.S. Supreme Court. The only significant exception to this new pattern of discretionary appellate jurisdiction is found under 28 U.S.C. section 1253 (dealing with three-judge federal district courts). So a direct appeal to the U.S. Supreme Court is allowed from three-judge district court cases (authorized in a limited number of situations, including the apportionment of legislative districts, some election campaign fund issues, Voting Rights Act issues, etc). All other review of federal appellate court decisions (except for certification issues under 28 U.S.C. section 1254(2)) and all review of state court decisions fall within the discretionary "certiorari" route.

REVIEW BY THE U.S. SUPREME COURT

I.
Original (trial) Jurisdiction
(exclusive; nonexclusive—28 U.S.C.1251)

II.
Appellate Review

A. Federal Court Decisions

(1) *district courts*

(a) appeal—28 U.S.C. 1253 (three-judge courts)

(2) *appellate courts*

(a) petition for certiorari—28 U.S.C. 1254(1)

(any case—but by tradition, cert. will not be granted if issue is one of state rather than federal law)

(b) certification—28 U.S.C. 1254(2)

B. State Court Decisions

(1) *highest state court in which review could be had*

(a) petition for certiorari—28 U.S.C. 1257

(if federal issue involved)

Chapter 18

Setting Aside the Judgment (Rule 60(b))

An additional opportunity for relief from an erroneous judgment is available from the trial court judge, in his or her discretion, under FRCP 60(b). See the chart entitled *Setting Aside the Judgment (FRCP 60(b))*. This remedy is extremely important because the right to move for a new trial or to appeal is limited strictly to defined periods (10 and 30 days respectively). Since some errors will not be discovered in time to raise in such a motion or appeal, a motion to vacate, or set aside, the judgment (under FRCP 60(b)), may be the only possible way to avoid what is claimed to be an erroneous judgment. Note, however, that such a motion is not supposed to be a substitute for an appeal and it is considered an extraordinary remedy.

The six grounds for relief under FRCP 60(b) can be divided into three categories. The *first* category contains grounds that cannot be raised more than one year after judgment has been entered (and must be raised within a reasonable time). The first ground is mistake, inadvertence, surprise or excusable neglect (under FRCP 60(b)(1)). (This ground is commonly used in trying to set aside a default judgment.) The second ground is newly discovered evidence which by due diligence could not have been discovered in time to move for a new trial under Rule 59(b) (under FRCP 60(b)(2)). This refers to evidence that was in existence at the time of the trial (see section 2859 of *Federal Practice and Procedure*, by Wright, Miller & Kane, at p. 302). The standards for such a motion, as stated in *Ag Pro, Inc. v. Sakraida*, 512 F.2d 141 (5th Cir. 1975), revd. on other grounds, 425 U.S. 273 (1976), are that it may not be granted unless (1) the evidence was discovered following the trial; (2) due diligence on the part of the movant to discover the new evidence is shown or may be inferred; (3) the evidence is not merely cumulative or impeaching; (4) the evidence is material; and (5) the evidence is such that a new trial would probably produce a new result. The final ground in this first category is fraud, misrepresentation, or other misconduct of an adverse party (under FRCP 60(b)(3)). The standards for such a motion, as set forth in *Rozier v. Ford Motor Co.*, 573 F.2d 1332 (5th Cir. 1978), are that the movant must prove by clear and convincing evidence the existence of such fraud, misreprentation, or other misconduct, and show that it prevented them from fully and fairly presenting its case.

The *second* category contains grounds that are also specific but only need to be brought within a reasonable time (so no particular time limitation). This includes the ground that the judgment is void (under FRCP 60(b)(4)). A motion based upon this ground is probably only available if the court that rendered it lacked subject matter jurisdiction over the case, personal jurisdiction over the defendant, or if it acted in a manner inconsistent with due process of law (see section 2862 of *Federal Practice and Procedure*, by Wright, Miller & Kane, at pp. 326-329). The second ground within this category is that the judgment has been satisfied, released, or discharged, or a prior judgment upon which it is based has been reversed or otherwise vacated, or it is no longer equitable that the judgment should have prospective application. The most common situations falling within this ground are when a prior judgment upon which claim or issue preclusion was based has been reversed or when a permanent injunction needs to be modified.

The *third* category includes the single ground of any other reason justifying relief from the operation of the judgment (under FRCP 60(b)(6)). This category cannot be used to avoid the timing restrictions for new trials, appeals, or motions under FRCP 60(b)(1), (2), or (3). Relief is limited to cases presenting "extraordinary circumstances" or grounds *other* than those listed in FRCP 60(b)(1)-(5). (See section 2864, *Federal Practice and Procedure*, by Wright, Miller & Kane.)

Note, also, the second to last sentence of FRCP 60(b), which allows motions to set aside a judgment for fraud upon the court.

SETTING ASIDE THE JUDGMENT
(FRCP 60(b))
Motion to Vacate, or Set Aside Judgment
(Extraordinary Remedy; Not Substitute for Appeal; Filed with the Trial Court Judge; Discretionary Decision)

The Six Grounds for Relief Under FRCP 60(b)
Can Be Divided Into Three Categories:

(1) Grounds that cannot be raised more than one year after judgment has been entered (and within a reasonable time):

- **60(b)(1)**—mistake, inadvertence, surprise, or excusable neglect (e.g. used to try to set aside a default judgment)

- **60(b)(2)**—newly discovered evidence which by due diligence could not have been discovered in time to move for a new trial under FRCP 59(b)

    (Such evidence must have been in existence at the time of the trial; *see standards for motion in Ag Pro, Inc. v. Sakraida,* 512 F.2d 141 (5th Cir.1975), revd. on other grounds, 425 U.S. 273 (1976))

- **60(b)(3)**—fraud (whether heretofore denominated intrinsic or extrinsic), misrepresentation, or other misconduct of an adverse party

    (*See Rozier v. Ford Motor Co.,* 573 F.2d 1332 (5th Cir. 1978)):

    - must prove by clear and convincing evidence the existence of such fraud, misrepresentation, or other misconduct, and

    - show that it prevented the moving party from fully and fairly presenting its case)

(2) Grounds that are also specific but only need to be brought within a reasonable time—(no particular time limitation)

- **60(b)(4)**—the judgment is void

    (This ground probably only available when the first court lacked subject matter jurisdiction over the case, personal jurisdiction over the defendant, or if it acted in a manner inconsistent with due process of law.)

- **60(b)(5)**—the judgment has been satisfied, released, or discharged, or a prior judgment upon which it is based has been reversed or otherwise vacated, or it is no longer equitable that the judgment should have prospective application

    (e.g. reversal of prior judgment upon which claim or issue preclusion was based, or need to modify permanent injunction)

SETTING ASIDE THE JUDGMENT, cont.

(3) The broadest category—**60(b)(6)**—under which relief must be sought within a reasonable time and which covers "any other reason justifying relief from the operation of the judgment"

- (This category cannot be used to avoid the timing restrictions for new trials, appeals, or motions under FRCP 60(b)(1), (2), or (3). Relief is limited to what are deemed cases presenting "extraordinary circumstances" or presenting grounds other than those listed in FRCP 60(b)(1) - (5).)

(See, also, the second to last sentence of FRCP 60(b), allowing motions to set aside a judgment for fraud upon the court.)

Chapter 19

Restraints on Subsequent Litigation

After a final judgment has been rendered in a case, common law principles generally prevent the re-litigation of the claims or issues raised in that case. The two relevant principles are called *claim preclusion* (or res judicata) and *issue preclusion* (or collateral estoppel). See the chart entitled *Attempts to Relitigate Claims or Issues* and *Issue Preclusion Examples*.

The first chart covers both claim and issue preclusion. The doctrine of claim preclusion was described in *Saylor v. Lindsley*, 391 F.2d 965 (2d Cir. 1968) as follows: A valid, final judgment rendered on the merits, constitutes an absolute bar to a subsequent action between the same parties, or those in privity with them, upon the same claim (or cause of action) or demand. It operates to bind the parties (and their privies) both as to issues actually litigated and determined in the first suit and those grounds or issues which might have been, but were not, actually raised and decided in that action. (In other words, the claim or cause of action must be brought all at once — no splitting of a claim or cause of action is allowed — and a litigant has only one opportunity to have it decided.) This is a fairly complicated topic, and each of its elements have been interpreted by case law. It is important that these cases should be consulted prior to attempting to bring a second lawsuit on some or all of the same issues raised in the first suit.

The doctrine of issue preclusion has been described in the *Restatement (Second) of Judgments, section 27* as follows: When an issue of fact or law is actually litigated and determined by a valid and final judgment and the determination is essential to the judgment, (then) the determination is conclusive in a subsequent action between the (same) parties, or those in privity with them, whether on the same or a different claim. (Note that there are some exceptions with respect to the same party rule.) Like claim preclusion, issue preclusion is a complicated area and case law offers interpretations of the various elements of the doctrine.

Because the topic of issue preclusion can be particularly difficult, a second chart is included in this chapter. See the chart entitled *Issue Preclusion Examples*. Under I, two examples are given of "mutual use" of issue preclusion. This means that the same parties are involved in both cases. As noted, we are also assuming that a different claim is involved in the second suit (or it is a state with no compulsory counterclaim rule), but the same issue is being raised. For example, in example IA, A sues B and B wins. In the second suit, when B sues A on a different claim, B may use his previous win on the same issue *offensively* against A (meaning to help prove his case). This is fair because the same parties were involved in the same case in which this issue was first decided (and we are assuming all of the other elements of issue preclusion have been met). The same is true for example IB, regarding defensive use of issue preclusion (to help defend the case). In either situation, the result of the previous determination of the issue in the first suit will be applied in the second suit as well (without relitigating it).

Section II of the chart illustrates nonmutual use of issue preclusion. In these situations issue preclusion is attempted to be used against someone who was a party to the first suit, but *by* a person who was *not* a party the first time around. Non-mutual issue preclusion is allowed is some jurisdictions and not allowed in others. Even in those jurisdictions that allow it, however, different results may occur in particular cases because of the discretionary standards applied. Nonmutual, defensive use (see example IIA) involves a non-party to the first suit using it against a party to the first suit — in order to help defend himself in the second suit. This is frequently allowed to avoid the situation where a party to the first suit decides to sue one defendant at a time in order to attempt to get a better result. There is a desire to protect the new defendant from such harassing litigation. Nonmutual, offensive use, however, is more problematic. In this situation (illustrated by example IIB), a non-party is using issue preclusion to affirmatively prove his case. As explained in *Parklane Hosiery Co. v. Shore*, 439 U.S. 322 (1979), this can cause difficulties because its use does not promote judicial economy the same way defensive use does, and its use may be unfair to the defendant. Case law on this issue should be consulted.

The issue preclusion examples listed under **IIC** (Violation of Due Process) are situations which are *not* allowed. In cases in which issue preclusion is asserted (in the second case) against someone who was not a party to the first action (and not in privity with such a party), the Due Process Clause (as well as simple fairness) prevents its application because the non-party must be given one opportunity to be heard. This is true whether issue preclusion is attempted to be used against a non-party *defensively* or *offensively*. In either instance, it is not permitted.

ATTEMPTS TO RELITIGATE CLAIMS OR ISSUES

CLAIM PRECLUSION
(or Res Judicata)

A valid, final judgment

- rendered on the merits
- constitutes an absolute bar to a subsequent action
- between the same parties, or those in privity with them,
- upon the same *claim* (cause of action) or *demand*.

AND it operates to bind the parties (and their privies) both as to

- issues *actually litigated* and determined in the first suit

AND

- those grounds or issues which *might have been,* but were not, actually raised and decided in that action.

(So no splitting of claims / causes of action is allowed)

(Saylor v. Lindsley,
391 F.2d 965 (2nd Cir. 1968))

ISSUE PRECLUSION
(or Collateral Estoppel)

When an *issue* of *fact* or *law*

- is actually litigated and determined
- by a valid and final judgment
- and the determination is essential to the judgment
- (then) the determination is conclusive in a subsequent action
- between the [same] parties, or those in privity with them

(*Note:* there are some exceptions to the same party rule)

- whether on the same or a different claim.

(Restatement (Second) of Judgments, section 27)

ISSUE PRECLUSION EXAMPLES

(assuming a different claim—or a state with no compulsory counterclaim rule—but the same issue in the second suit)

I. MUTUAL USE (same parties in both suits or their privies)

(A) Offensive Use

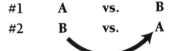

#1	A	vs.	B	(**B** wins)
#2	B	vs.	A	(**B** may use previous win on issue *offensively*)

(A) Defensive Use

#1	A	vs.	B	(**A** wins)
#2	B	vs.	A	(**A** may use previous win on issue *defensively*)

(If the same parties or their privies are involved, can use issue preclusion, or collateral estoppel, either offensively or defensively.)

II. NONMUTUAL USE

(A) Defensive Use (allowed in some jurisdictions)

#1	A	vs.	B	(**A** loses—e.g. based on its contributory negligence)
#2	A	vs.	C	(**C** relies on **A**'s loss—and is asserting it defensively against *party* to first suit)

(B) Offensive Use (allowed in some jurisdictions)

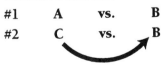

#1	A	vs.	B	(**B** loses)
#2	C	vs.	B	(**C** relies on **B**'s loss—and is asserting it offensively against a party to the first suit)

ISSUE PRECLUSION EXAMPLES, cont.

II. NONMUTUAL USE (cont.)

(C) Violation of Due Process
(asserting it against a non-party to the first suit)

(1) Defensive Use   (NO)

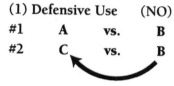

#1	**A**	vs.	**B**	(**B** wins)
#2	**C**	vs.	**B**	(**B** tries to rely on its win in the first case—defensively—but *cannot* do so since **C** was not a party to the first suit)

(2) Offensive Use   (NO)

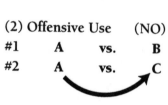

#1	**A**	vs.	**B**	(**A** wins)
#2	**A**	vs.	**C**	(**A**—offensively—tries to rely on its win in the first case, but *cannot* do so since **C** was not a party to the first suit)

Part II

Document Drafting Checklists

Checklist #1
Complaint

Caption (FRCP 10)   _____

   —Name of Court/Parties' Names
   and Addresses/Designation/
   Line for Case No./
   Line for Judge's Name

   —Jury Demand (FRCP 38)

Introductory Clause   _____

Introduction Paragraph   _____

Basis for Jurisdiction/Venue   _____
(FRCP 8(a)(1); see
28 U.S.C. sections 1331,
1332, 1367, 1391)

Description of Parties   _____

Background Facts

   —e.g. Contract/Personal   _____
   Injury/$ due

   —(Mention of Critical   _____
   Documents that are
   Attached, e.g. Lease)

   —Explanation of Damage/Costs   _____

Claims/Counts (FRCP 8(a)(2); 18; 20)

   —e.g. Contract (rent)   _____

   —e.g. Tort (property damage)   _____

Demand for Judgment (FRCP 8(a)(3))   _____

Signature Block   _____

   —Client's Name or Law Firm Name/
   Signature Line/Attorney's Name,
   Address, Telephone Number,
   Bar Registration Number

Jury Demand (FRCP 38)   _____
  (with separate signature)

Also Check:

Organization
  —Structure   _____
  —Clarity
      —Separation of Claims   _____
      —Separate Paragraphs   _____

Expression
  —Degree Unnecessary or Excess
    Facts/Law—or Too Few
    Allegations   _____
  —Language Used
      —Simple, Concise, Direct   _____
      —Consistent Terms   _____

Evidence of Theory of Case   _____
  (Tells a Story?)

(Include Summons)

Checklist #2
Pre-Answer Motions*

Notice of Hearing/Motion   _____

   —Identification of Motion/
   Time, Date, and Location
   of Hearing

Motions (FRCP 7(b))

   —*Identification of Request*   _____
   (e.g. to dismiss, FRCP 12(b)
   (1)-(7); for more definite
   statement, FRCP 12(e);
   to strike, FRCP 12(f))

   —*Identification of Grounds*   _____
   (including rule no./statute no.)

   —(reference to attached
   memorandum)   _____

**Memorandum (in Support/of Points
and Authorities)**

   —*Introduction*   _____
   (Brief description of case,
   motions being brought)

   —*Facts*   _____
   (with citations to sworn sources)

   —*Argument*   _____
   (legal and factual analysis
   in support of motions)

   —*Conclusion*   _____
   (summary of relief sought)

Proposed Order(s)   _____
   (for judge to sign,
   ruling in your favor
   on motions) (optional)

Certificate of Service   _____

    —Name and Address of Person Served/
    Method of Service/Date of Service/
    Identification of Document(s)
    Being Served

Include on Each Separate Document:

Caption   _____

    —Name of Court/Parties' Names
    and Addresses/Designation/
    Case No. or File No./
    Name of Judge

Date   _____

Signature Block   _____

    —Client's Name or Law Firm Name/
    Signature Line/Attorney's Name,
    Address, Telephone Number,
    Bar Registration Number

Also Check:

    —Structure/Clarity   _____

    —Accurate Use of Facts   _____

    —Citation of Proper Rules/   _____
    Standards/Case Law

    —Application of Law to Facts   _____

    —Degree Unnecessary/   _____
    Insufficient Arguments

    —Language—Degree of Wordiness/   _____
    Excessive Legalese

    —Persuasiveness/Appeal   _____

*With the exception of the proposed orders, these can be combined
into one document (with appropriate identification of such in the
caption) or be drafted as separate documents.

Checklist #3
Responses to Motions

Caption   _____

   —Name of Court/Parties' Names/
   Designation/Case No. or File No./
   Name of Judge

Memorandum in Response
   (making reference to exact
    title of motion)

   Content

   —*Introduction*   _____
   (Brief description of case,
   motions being opposed)

   —*Facts*   _____
   (with citations to sworn sources)

   —*Argument*   _____
   (legal and factual analysis
   supporting arguments
   against motions)

     (*Include*

     —identification of reasons
      for opposing motions

     —direct responses to
      opposing party's arguments)

   —*Conclusion*   _____
   (summary of relief sought,
   e.g. denial of motions)

Date   _____

Signature Block   _____

   —Client's Name or Law Firm Name/
   Signature Line/Attorney's Name,
   Address, Telephone Number,
   Bar Registration Number

Certificate of Service   _____

 —Name and Address of Person
  Served/Method of Service/Date of
  Service/Identification of
  Document(s) Being Served

Proposed Order(s)   _____

 (for judge to sign,
  ruling in your favor—
  denying motions) (optional)

Also Check for:

 —Clarity/Persuasiveness   _____

 —Accurate Use of Facts   _____

 —Citation of Proper Rules/   _____
  Standards/Case Law

 —Application of Law to Facts   _____

Checklist #4
Answer and Defendants' Claims

Caption (FRCP 10)   _____

   — Name of Court/Parties' Names/
     Designation/Case No. or File No./
     Name of Judge

   — Jury Demand (FRCP 38)

Introductory Clause   _____

Responses to Allegations in Complaint

   (Admit/Deny/Lack Sufficient Knowledge
     or Information) (FRCP 8(b))
   — Includes Response to *Each*   _____
     Allegation

   — Responses in Proper Form   _____

   — Appropriate Responses   _____

Affirmative Defenses

   (See FRCP 8(c); 12(b); case law)

   (*Examples:*

   — Failure to State a Claim   _____
     (FRCP 12(b)(6))?

   — Payment (paid for value)   _____
     (FRCP 8(c))?

   — Contributory Negligence   _____
     (FRCP 8(c))?

   — Estoppel (FRCP 8(c))?   _____

   — Failure of Consideration   _____
     (FRCP 8(c))?

Counterclaims (with structure like
   Complaint) (FRCP 13(a),(b))

   — e.g. where D seeks damages   _____
     from P (as in claim for
     breach of contract/
     personal injury)

Cross—Claims (with structure like Complaint) (FRCP 13(g))

　　—e.g. Where Two Ds in Original Suit and One D Wants to Sue the Other D in the Same Suit　　_____

Third—Party Claims (with structure like Complaint) (FRCP 14)

　　—e.g. Where D Wants to Bring in Third—Party D Who Is or May Be Liable to Him　　_____

Demand for Judgment　　_____

Date　　_____

Signature Block　　_____

　　—Client's Name or Law Firm Name/ Signature Line/Attorney's Name, Address, Telephone Number, Bar Registration Number

Jury Demand (FRCP 38) (with separate signature)　　_____

Certificate of Service　　_____

　　—Name/Address of Person Served/ Method of Service/Date of Service/ Identification of Document(s) Being Served

Also Check:

Organization

　　—Structure/Clarity　　_____

Expression

　　—Degree Unnecessary/ Insufficient Allegations　　_____

　　—Language—Degree of Wordiness/ Excessive Legalese　　_____

Checklist #5
Report of Parties' Planning Meeting (Form 35)
(See Form 35; FRCP 26(f))

Caption   _____

   —Name of Court/Parties' Names/
   Designation/Case No. or File No./
   Name of Judge

Content

   —*Contains All Elements in Form*   _____

   1. *Date/Place of FRCP 26(f) Meeting; Persons Attending*
   2. *Date of Disclosures Under FRCP 26(a)(1)*
   3. *Proposed Joint Discovery Plan* (including subjects of discovery; discovery cut-off date(s); maximum number of interrogatories and requests for admission, and response times; maximum number of depositions and length restrictions; dates expert reports due; times or intervals for supplementing discovery)
   4. *Other Items* (including whether requesting court conference prior to scheduling order; month and year pretrial conference requested; cut-off dates for both parties to amend pleadings and join parties; cut-off date for filing of dispositive motions; likelihood of settlement/suggestion of ADR procedure(s); due dates for filing final witness and exhibit lists, and for making objections to such lists; date by which the case will be ready for trial; projected length of trial)

   —Drafting: Clear/Simply Stated   _____

   —Reasonableness and Consistency
   of Dates/Time Limitations/
   Discovery Limits   _____

Date   _____

Signature Block (for both counsel)

    ——Client's Name or Law Firm Name/
Signature Line/Attorney's Name,
Address, Telephone Number,
Bar Registration Number

Checklist #6
Initial Disclosures
(FRCP 26(a)(1))

Caption _____

   —Name of Court/Parties' Names/
Designation/Case No. or File No./
Name of Judge

Content
   (Accurate and Complete
Information Given?)

   —*26(a)(1)(A)— Witnesses* _____
(persons with discoverable
information) (provide
name/address/phone/
subject of information)
(**note limitation:** applies to
individuals likely to have
discoverable information
relevant to *disputed facts
alleged with particularity
in the pleadings*)

   —*26(a)(1)(B)— Documents/Things* _____
(description or copies)

   (**note same limitation as above**)

   —*26(a)(1)(C)— Damage
Computation* _____
(and underlying documents)

   —*26(a)(1)(D)— Insurance
Agreements* _____

Date _____

Signature Block   _____

    —Client's Name or Law Firm Name/
    Signature Line/Attorney's Name,
    Address, Telephone Number,
    Bar Registration Number

Certificate of Service   _____

    —Name and Address of Person Served/
    Method of Service/Date of Service/
    Identification of Document(s)
    Being Served

Also Check Drafting:

    —Clear/Simply Stated?   _____

(**Note** continuing duty to supplement, under FRCP 26(e)(1).)

Checklist #7
Interrogatories
(FRCP 33)

Caption   _____

  —Name of Court/Parties' Names/
  Designation/Case No. or File No./
  Name of Judge

Introduction

  —Introductory Sentence   _____
  (including citation of FRCP 30
  and due date for answers)

  —Definitions   _____

  —Instructions   _____

Content (case-specific)   _____

  —Examples of Categories:

    —Questions Re: Parties/Witnesses/Persons
    with Knowledge

    —Questions Re: Causes of Actions/Defenses

    —Questions Re: Injuries/Damages

    —Questions Re: Trial Experts/Exhibits

    —Questions Designed to Identify Additional
    Relevant Documents

Date   _____

Signature of Counsel   _____

  —Client's Name or Law Firm Name/
  Signature Line/Attorney's Name,
  Address, Telephone Number,
  Bar Registration Number

Certificate of Service _____

   —Name and Address of Person Served/
   Method of Service/Date of Service/
   Identification of Document(s)
   Being Served

Also Check Drafting:

   —No Compound/Multiple
   Questions? _____

   —No Questions Capable of _____
   Being Answered "Yes" or "No"?

   —No Clearly Objectionable _____
   Questions?

   —Simple, Clear, Direct Language? _____

Checklist #8
Answers to Interrogatories

Caption   _____

    —Name of Court/Parties' Names/
    Designation/Case No. or File No./
    Name of Judge

Content (FRCP 33(b), (d))

    For Each Interrogatory:

        —Repeat the Interrogatory   _____

        —Give Accurate/Complete
        Information   _____

        and/or

        Make an Objection

Date   _____

Signature Block (for Attorney)   _____

    —Client's Name or Law Firm Name/
    Signature Line/Attorney's Name,
    Address, Telephone Number,
    Bar Registration Number

Oath/Signature of Party   _____

    (verification of truth of answers)

Certificate of Service   _____

    —Name and Address of Person Served/
    Method of Service/Date of Service/
    Identification of Document(s)
    Being Served

Also Check:

Drafting:

    —Answers Stated Well?   _____

    —Clear?   _____

Judgment/Strategy/Ethics:

  —Evasive Answers?   _____

  —Too Much Info Given/
  Too Little Info Given?   _____

  —Not Stated in Positive Light?   _____

  —Improper Objections/
  Failure to Make Appropriate
  Objections?

(*Note:* See FRCP 26(e)(2) re: continuing duty to supplement when answer becomes incomplete or incorrect in some material respect.)

Checklist #9
Requests for Production
(FRCP 34)

Caption   _____

   —Name of Court/Parties' Names/
   Designation/Case No. or File No./
   Name of Judge

Introduction

   —Introduction: _____

      —Cite FRCP 34

      —Indicate Response Time
      (30 days)

      —Indicate Time, Place, Manner
      of Production (either as
      specified, or to be mutually
      agreed upon)

   —Definitions   _____

   —Instructions   _____

Specific Requirements

   —The Requests Must Set   _____
   Forth, Either by Individual
   Item or by *Category*, the
   Items to be Inspected

   —The Items Requested Must   _____
   be Described with
   Reasonable Particularity

Tangible Things/Premises   _____
(to be inspected)

Documents Requested _____

- e.g. Those Listed in Initial
  Disclosures
- e.g. Those Identified in
  Interrogatory Answers
- e.g. Other Specific Requests
  (statements/photos/inspection
  reports/bills/notices/contracts/etc.)

Date _____

Signature Block _____

- Client's Name or Law Firm Name/
  Signature Line/Attorney's Name,
  Address, Telephone Number,
  Bar Registration Number

Certificate of Service _____

- Name and Address of Person Served/
  Method of Service/Date of Service/
  Identification of Document(s)
  Being Served

Also Check Drafting:

- No Clearly Objectionable
  Requests? _____
- Simple, Clear, Direct Language? _____

Checklist #10
Responses to Requests for Production
(FRCP 34)

Caption   _____

    —Name of Court/Parties' Names/
    Designation/Case No. or File No./
    Name of Judge

Introductory Clause   _____

Responses (FRCP 34(b))

    —Written Response as Well   _____
    as Production of Documents?

    —Separate Response or   _____
    Objection Made to Each
    Request?

    —Accurate/Complete?   _____

    —Documents Produced as Kept   _____
    in the Usual Course of
    Business *Or* Organized
    and Labeled to Correspond
    With the Categories in
    the Request?

Date   _____

Signature Block   _____

    —Client's Name or Law Firm Name/
    Signature Line/Attorney's Name,
    Address, Telephone Number,
    Bar Registration Number

Certificate of Service   _____

    —Name and Address of Person Served/
    Method of Service/Date of Service/
    Identification of Document(s)
    Being Served

Also Check Drafting/Judgment:

— Well-Stated?   _____

— Appropriate Responses/
   Objections?   _____

(*Note:* See FRCP 26(e)(2) re: continuing duty to supplement when answer becomes incomplete or incorrect in some material respect.)

Checklist #11
Requests for Admissions
(FRCP 36)

Caption _____

    —Name of Court/Parties' Names/
    Designation/Case No. or
    File No./Name of Judge

Introduction

    —Introduction: _____

        —Cite FRCP 36

        —Indicate Response Time
        (30 days)

    —Definitions _____

    —Instructions _____

Requests _____

    Asking the Other Party to
    Admit (for the Purposes of
    the Pending Action Only)—

        —The *Truth* of Matters _____
        Relating to Statements or
        Opinions of Fact, or of
        Application of Law to Fact

        and/or

        —The *Genuineness* of
        Documents _____

Date _____

Signature Block _____

    —Client's Name or Law Firm Name/
    Signature Line/Attorney's Name,
    Address, Telephone Number,
    Bar Registration Number

Certificate of Service　　　　　　　　＿＿＿＿＿＿＿＿＿＿

　　—Name and Address of Person
　　Served/Method of Service/
　　Date of Service/Identification
　　of Document(s) Being Served

Also Check Drafting:

　　—Requests Stated with Reasonable
　　Particularity?　　　　　　　　　＿＿＿＿＿＿＿＿＿＿

　　—Simple, Clear, Direct Language?　＿＿＿＿＿＿＿＿＿＿

Checklist #12
Responses to Requests for Admissions
(FRCP 36)

Caption _____

 — Name of Court/Parties' Names/
  Designation/Case No. or File No./
  Name of Judge

Introductory Clause _____

Responses (FRCP 36) _____

 — Response to _Every_ Request?
  (Since It Will Be Deemed
  Admitted if No Timely Response)

 — Either Admit, Deny, Qualify
  the Response, or Object?

Date _____

Signature Block _____

 — Client's Name or Law Firm Name/
  Signature Line/Attorney's Name,
  Address, Telephone Number,
  Bar Registration Number

Certificate of Service _____

 — Name and Address of Person Served/
  Method of Service/Date of Service/
  Identification of Document(s)
  Being Served

(_Note:_ See FRCP 26(e)(2) re: continuing duty to supplement when answer becomes incomplete or incorrect in some material respect.)

Checklist #13
Motion for Physical/Mental Examination
(FRCP 35)

Motion (FRCP 35; 7(b)(1))

— *Identification of Request*   _____

  (for physical or mental
  examination of opposing party,
  or person in custody or under
  legal control of that party)

— *Identification of Grounds*   _____

  — person's physical or
   mental condition is in
   controversy

  — good cause exists (relevant
   and you need the information)

— *Specification of Date, Time,*   _____
Place, Manner, Conditions,
and Scope of Examination

— *Designation of Physician Who* _____
Will Perform Examination

— (reference to attached
memorandum)   _____

**Memorandum (in Support/of Points
and Authorities)**

— *Introduction*   _____
(Brief description of case,
motions being brought)

— *Facts*   _____
(with citations to sworn sources)

— *Argument*   _____
(legal and factual analysis
in support of above grounds)

— *Conclusion*   _____
(summary of relief sought)

Proposed Order _____
    (for judge to sign,
      ruling in your favor
      on motion) (optional)

Certificate of Service _____
    —Name and Address of Person Served/
    Method of Service/Date of Service/
    Identification of Document(s)
    Being Served

Include on Each Separate Document:

Caption _____
    —Name of Court/Parties' Names
    and Addresses/Designation/
    Case No. or File No./
    Name of Judge

Date _____

Signature Block _____
    —Client's Name or Law Firm Name/
    Signature Line/Attorney's Name,
    Address, Telephone Number,
    Bar Registration Number

(*Note:* See separate chart re: Responses to Motions)

Checklist #14
Notice of Deposition
(FRCP 30(b))

Caption   _____

   —Name of Court/Parties' Names/
   Designation/Case No. or
   File No./Name of Judge

Content

   —Cite FRCP 30   _____

   —Include Name and *Address*   _____
   of Deponent

   —Date, Time and Specific   _____
   Location of Deposition

Date   _____

Signature Block   _____

   —Client's Name or Law Firm Name/
   Signature Line/Attorney's Name,
   Address, Telephone Number,
   Bar Registration Number

Certificate of Service

   —(upon opposing counsel)   _____

   —Proper Form   _____

      —Name and Address of
      Person Served/Method of Service/
      Date of Service/Identification
      of Document(s) Being Served

Checklist #15
Joint Deposition Notice/Subpoena

Joint Deposition Notice

Caption   _____

    —Name of Court/Parties' Names/
    Designation/Case No. or File No./
    Name of Judge

Content

    —Cite FRCP 30   _____

    —Include Name and *Address*   _____
    of Deponent

    —Date, Time and Specific   _____
    Location of Deposition

Date   _____

Signature Block (of *both* attorneys)   _____

    —Client's Name or Law Firm Name/
    Signature Line/Attorney's Name,
    Address, Telephone Number,
    Bar Registration Number

(No Certificate of Service Necessary)

Subpoena*

    —Deposition Format   _____

    —Cite FRCP 45   _____

    —Include Name and Address   _____
    of Deponent

    —Date, Time and Specific   _____
    Location of Deposition

    —*Include Language From*   _____
    FRCP 45(c) & (d)

—Date   _____

—Signature Block   _____

    —Client's Name or Law Firm Name/
       Signature Line/Attorney's Name,
       Address, Telephone Number,
       Bar Registration Number

*Required if non-party deponent; court form can be used.

Checklist #16
Preparing a Deposition Outline

Deposition Outline (for Depositions under FRCP 30)

Introduction

— Intro of Self/Others   _____

— Intro of Depo/Depo Process   _____
(Been Deposed Before?)

— *OATH*   _____

— Personal Data/Background   _____

List of Topics About Which   _____
to Question Deponent

Use of Exhibit(s) During Deposition

— Ask if Accurate Depiction/   _____
Original or True and Correct
Copy

— Mark as Exhibit/Describe on   _____
Record/Ask to Be Made Part
of Record

— Have Deponent Make   _____
Meaningful Marks On It
(During Depo)

Concluding Questions

— Want to Add/Change Anything?   _____

— Waive Reading/Signing   _____
of Transcript?

Also:

Prepare for Problem-Solving During Depo, e.g.

— Obtain Answers to Questions   _____

— Obtain Understandable/   _____
Oral Responses

—Remain in Control of
Deposition/Deponent   _____

—Pin Down Witness (On
Important Points)   _____

To Be Determined Prior to Deposition

—Theory of Your Case?   _____

—How Does This Deponent Fit
Within This Theory?   _____

—What Do You Hope to Get
From This Deponent?   _____

Checklist #17
Outline for Preparing a Deponent
(for a FRCP 30 Deposition)

Explanation of Process Generally   _____
  (Including Objections)

General Advice Re: Responding   _____
  to Questions

Discussion of Responses to All   _____
  Anticipated Questions

Explanation of Strategy/Theory of Case   _____

Ideas for Specific Information to be   _____
  Revealed for Potential Settlement/
  Other Purposes

Checklist #18
Pretrial Motions

(**EXAMPLES:** Motions in Limine (under Federal Rules of
Evidence); for Summary Judgment (FRCP 56); to Consolidate
(FRCP 42(a)); to Sever (FRCP 42(b), 21))

Motions (FRCP 7(b))

— *Identification of Request*   _____
(e.g. for summary judgment)

— *Identification of Grounds*   _____
(including rule no./statute no.)

— (reference to attached
memorandum)   _____

**Memorandum (in Support/of Points
and Authorities)**

— *Introduction*   _____
(Brief description of case,
motions being brought)

— *Facts*   _____
(with citations to sworn sources)

— *Argument*   _____
(legal and factual analysis
in support of motions)

— *Conclusion*   _____
(summary of relief sought)

Proposed Order(s)   _____
(for judge to sign,
ruling in your favor
on motions) (optional)

Certificate of Service   _____

— Name and Address of Person Served/
Method of Service/Date of Service/
Identification of Document(s)
Being Served

Include on Each Separate Document:

Caption

    —Name of Court/Parties' Names
    and Addresses/Designation/
    Case No. or File No./
    Name of Judge

Date

Signature Block

    —Client's Name or Law Firm Name/
    Signature Line/Attorney's Name,
    Address, Telephone Number,
    Bar Registration Number

Also check:

    —Structure/Clarity

    —Accurate Use of Facts

    —Citation of Proper Rules/
    Standards/Case Law

    —Application of Law to Facts

    —Degree Unnecessary/
    Insufficient Arguments

    —Language—Degree of Wordiness/
    Excessive Legalese

    —Persuasiveness/Appeal

*With the exception of the proposed orders, these
can be combined into one document (with appropriate
identification of such in the caption) or be drafted
as separate documents.

(*Note:* See separate chart re: Responses to Motions)

Checklist #19
Joint Pretrial Statements
(See FRCP 16; Court's Instructions)

Caption   _____

— Name of Court/Parties' Names/
Designation/Case No. or File No./
Name of Judge

Introductory Clause   _____

Content*

— *Stipulated Facts*   _____

— *Issues of Fact*   _____
(to be tried)

— *Issues of Law*   _____
(to be tried)

— *Witness List*   _____
(for each side)

— *Exhibit List*   _____
(for each side)

— *Jury Instructions*   _____
(see FRCP 51)

Date   _____

Signature Block (for *both* counsel)   _____

— Client's Name or Law Firm Name/
Signature Line/Attorney's Name,
Address, Telephone Number
Bar Registration Number

Also Check Drafting:

— Clearly Stated?   _____

— Concise, But Complete?   _____

*The content may vary somewhat according to the particular
judge's preferences.

(*No Certificate of Service Necessary*)

Checklist #20
Settlement Agreement Checklist

Contract Format   _____

Names of Parties   _____

Mention of Pending Suit   _____

Consideration/Releases   _____

Specification of What
  Each Party is to Do   _____

    —Re: execution of settlement
    (e.g. payment of funds—
    when? how? in what form?)

    —Re: disposition of lawsuit/
    payment of costs (e.g. filing
    of stipulation of dismissal

    —who will do it? when?
    in what form?)

Confidentiality Provision   _____

Denial of Liability Provision
  (if desired)   _____

Provision Re: This Constituting
  the Entire Agreement of the Parties   _____

Date   _____

Signature of Parties and Counsel   _____

Checklist #21
Court Document Disposing of Settled Case

Caption   _____

    —Name of Court/Parties' Names/
    Designation/Case No. or File No./
    Name of Judge

Content

    —*Cites Applicable Rules*   _____
    (e.g. FRCP 41(a)(1)(ii), (c))

    —*Deals with Payment of Costs*   _____
    (e.g. each side pays own)

    —*Specifies Effect of Document*   _____
    (e.g. dismissal of *all*
    claims *with prejudice*)

Date   _____

Signature Block (for both attorneys)   _____

    —Client's Name or Law Firm Name/
    Signature Line/Attorney's Name,
    Address, Telephone Number,
    Bar Registration Number

(*No Certificate of Service Necessary*)

Index of Federal Rules
and Statutes

Federal Rules of Civil Procedure

Federal Rules of Appellate Procedure

Federal Statutes